PRAYERS

FOR

DELIVERANCE FROM

CRACK COCAINE

AND

ALCOHOL ADDICTION

by

Christian Willie J. Henderson

1

Introduction

There are numerous books written on prayer but this is the only one that focuses entirely on teaching the reader how to pray entirely *for deliverance* from crack cocaine, heroin, crystal meth, marijuana, alcohol and sexual sins that accompany drug addiction.

The reason that our children, neighborhoods, and households are challenged with drug addiction and drug dealing is because society has wavered from *"faithful and effectual fervent prayer"* (Js.5:15-17) and now depend on doctors and professional counseling to restore and help the lost deal with the addictions and temptations that surrounds them. To make matters worse our jails and prisons are not overcrowded with addicts, drug dealers, murderers, thieves and robbers simply because of the crimes they commit, but mainly because those committing the crimes have not been educated, taught how to follow the example that Christ set for mankind in Luke 4:1-13 and pray for deliverance from their mindset, drugs and others challenges that cause them to sin against God's commandments. Yes, there are 13 step and other programs that suggest that struggling addicts refer to the name, "higher power", but truth be told, **"There's no other name except the name Jesus** associated with the implement of prayer **that will result in the deliverance and salvation of man!"** *(See Acts 16:18; 4:10,12).*

The Bible clearly tells us that **"Christ defeated temptation, Satan by a means open to his humblest** follower, **THE INTELLIGENT USE OF THE WORD OF GOD".** *(See Matt.4: 1, Scofield Study Bible footnotes),*

Copy right © 2014 by Minister Willie J. Henderson.

All rights reserved. No part of this book may be reproduced or transmitted in any form or by any means, electronic or mechanical, including photocopying, recording, or by any information storage and retrieval system, without the written permission of the Publisher, "My Father's House Shelter & Drug Deliverance Residence, Columbia, S.C. 29209.

Check Out This Very Brief Testimonial Of Why God Had Me To Begin The Crack Cocaine Deliverance Ministry: at:

http://qiksocial.com/story/6/from-a-20-year-homeless-crackhead-to-a-minister/

A percentage of all book sales will go towards the future and foundation of the *My Father's House Shelter & Drug Deliverance Residence* which is dedicated to housing, feeding, clothing and teach individuals who are sincere about getting off drugs, re-dedicating their life how to Christ and once again becoming productive members of society how overcome the temptations to use, to steal, to prostitute themselves or commit other related sins connected to the addiction by *"following the example that Christ set for mankind in Luke 4:1-3 and apply the power of the written Word of God."*

Check Out This Very Brief Testimonial Of Why God Had Me To Begin The Crack Cocaine Deliverance Ministry: at:

http://qiksocial.com/story/6/from-a-20-year-homeless-crackhead-to-a-minister/

To sow a seed of any amount visit:

http://qiksocial.com/fundraising/3/my-father-039-s-house-shelter-christian-drug-recovery/

Email me at: *christianwilliej@gmail.com*

This book was printed in the United States of America.

For prayer call **(803) 237-0205 or (803) 297-3509,**

Also order books from church website at:
www.christdeliveredme.yolasite.com
GOOGLE: Christian Willie J. Henderson or Minister Willie J. Henderson

"Brethren, my heart's desire and prayer to God is that you might be saved"

(Rom.10:1)

There's no coincidence that you're reading this book at this time. Maybe you have a family member, friend, husband, wife, daughter, son, mother or dad who's struggling with alcohol and crack cocaine addiction, or maybe it's you. Whatever the case may be God has answered your prayers by way of this book. He knows that you're sick and tired of the heart ache, pain, and misery that is associated with the addiction. God knows that you're tired of living with someone who's causing you stress because they're on crack; God knows that you're tired of hurting the ones who love you the most, going in and out of the rehabs, being homeless, prostituting yourself; not being able to hold on to a job, pay rent, pawning the car, your television, tired of looking into the mirror and seeing how pathetic you really are! And so it's why He has blessed you this book.

This book is the result of a 20 year struggle I had with crack cocaine, heroin, alcohol, marijuana, and other drugs. I have now been ministering for years to others who are struggling to be free from the immoralities of crack cocaine, but prior to that I was also subjected to crack cocaine addiction, homeless, sleeping in the woods, underneath bridges, in old abandoned cars, bouncing from state to state, and from one homeless shelter to another, going in and out of jail and prison... I was reduced to eating out of restaurant trash, robbing, stealing, begging, and committing other low life abominations to acquire crack cocaine. I suffered years of being paranoid and afraid for my life because I either owed the drug dealers money or stole from them. I like so many naive others was *deceived*

6

into thinking that the curiosity of crack cocaine would be quickly resolved, but that day of inquisitiveness stole 20 years of my life as my struggle for deliverance remained in limbo.

Then one day after awakening from an unsuccessful suicide attempt I was sitting in the park reading the Bible and the Holy Spirit directed me to Ephesians 6:12 and Luke 4:1-12. It was in the book of Ephesians where God revealed to me that my battle for *deliverance* and *reason for addiction* was because "my fight was against those rebellious angelic spirits who were expelled from heaven into the earth's atmosphere" (Rev.12:9.12,17;18:2) that "possess" (Matt.4:24; 8:16; Acts 19:12-16), "promote and express their own characteristics of sin and rebellion in those they victimize" (See Eph.2:2; Acts 5:3; Jn.13:2).

The book of Luke 4:1-12 is what really led to my deliverance. While reading the gospel I noticed that each time Jesus was tempted by the devil he **immediately** responded, **"It is written",** followed by the appropriate verse of scripture. Well, after many failed attempts at various drug rehabs, I decide to follow Christ's example and surely the pathetic addiction to crack cocaine finally came to its end! It was soon after my deliverance that "the Holy Spirit of God inspired me" (2Tim.3:16) to write down the prayers, verses and scriptures that I used to defeat the devils suggestions and overcome the temptations to use which became this book: **"Crack Cocaine Let my People Go; Appropriate Prayer Results In Deliverance"**.

The Spirit motivated words of this book are written with the intent of teaching those who are struggling with crack cocaine, other drugs, and immoral living how to subdue temptations and cravings by doing what Jesus did when was being tempted: Retaliate with "the

7

sword of the Spirit" (Eph.6:17), "which written Word of God" (Lk. 4:1,3,4,6,8,12).

Yes, **the written word of God** is the very weapon Jesus used against Satan's temptations in the wilderness! When a person, as Christ did, quotes the written word in the face of adversity they are actually *allowing the supernatural power of God, Jesus to voice Himself* through them in the face of adversity! The Bible verifies that is was indeed *"the supernatural power of God working through Jesus"* (Matt.12:28) that gave him his power to cast out devils. And just as *the Supernatural Administering Power of God* rested upon *"Elijah"* (1Kg. 18:46; Js.5:17), *"Paul"* (Acts 19: 11-12), *"John"* (Jn.1:6), *"Jesus"* (Lk.11:20), and especially *"the seventy followers of Christ which gave them all power of the devil and to do other works"* (Lk.10:17) that same power of God the Holy Spirit is available to you! It's the power and authority that the devil has been hoping that you'd never discover! What is it? It's the **"Holy Spirit of God and the Power of the Written Word"** working together to bring to life and create in you **"the Christian character that self-effort cannot accomplish alone"** (see Gal. 5:16, 22-26 LBV).

Through Christ, *"who is the Word of God"* (Jn.1:1, 10; 14) there's a greater binding of sin than it was in the beginning of creation. The first Adam was instructed to subdue the earth (Gen.1:26; 28); the second Adam, Christ was instructed to subdue not only the earth but *"the spirit realm also"* (1Jn.3:8; 1Cor.15:45-48). The Bible declares, **"Blessed be the God and Father of our Lord Jesus Christ, WHO HAS BLESSED US WITH ALL SPIRITUAL BLESSINGS in heavenly places in Christ...** (Eph.1:3,5). What does that verse mean? It means that God has blessed you with *"the same authority, power and spiritual blessings"* **that** He blessed Christ with to overcome temptations, influences and evils of the spirit realm! My friend, the phrase *"spiritual blessings..."* in the verse above

8

simply refers to the power and authority that "faith in the Written Word will accomplish" (Matt.9:29; 21:21; Lk.7:50) for those who believe that *"God's word will not return them void but accomplish all that they sent it out to do for them!"* (Isa. 55:10-11).

Just as a car, bicycle, piece of furniture, machinery, or any other piece of equipment comes with an instruction manual from the manufacturer to put it together, repair it, or keep it functioning properly the Bible is man's instruction manual from God, who is our manufacturer. In it *are INSTRUCTIONS for living, keeping our lives running properly, putting our lives together, and repairing life's damages"* (2Tim.3:16-17 LBV).

I've Prayed But It Seems It's Not Working For Me

The problem that I've noticed in reference to *deliverance,* or healing, is that many people are sincerely praying but referring to the wrong verses of Scripture when it comes to repairing the damage that they're suffering, and as a result their deliverance hangs in limbo. The Bible clearly tells us that **"Christ defeated Satan by a means open to his humblest follower, THE INTELLIGENT USE OF THE WORD OF GOD"** (see Matt.4: 1, Scofield Bible study notes), and just like Christ, our example, who prayed, *quoted* the **appropriate** verses of scripture in the face of adversity (Lk.4:1-13), God wants us to likewise refer to His Written Word, His promises, then **"put him in remembrance of his word that we too may be "justified" set free,** (Isa.43:26), or so that he can begin making repairs. When people who are struggling are set free, *justified* **by the Word of God**, from their addiction to crack cocaine, or their drug of choice communities, families, neighborhoods, and households benefit from their restoration and deliverance!

9

Table of Contents

1

The Unseen War Against Influential Demon Spirits

For we are not wrestling with flesh and blood {CONTENDING ONLY WITH PHYSICAL OPPONENTS}, **but against despotisms** *(somatic entity deposited by a spiritual process)...* against the spirit forces of wickedness in the heavenly (supernatural) sphere" (Eph.6:12 AMP). What is a spirit? A spirit is simply a character trait influenced either by *"God's Holy Spirit"* (see Gal.5:16, 22-25) or the *"influence and character traits of the devil's evil, rebellious spirit"* (Eph.2:2; Rev.13:6 CEV, 1Chr.21:1; Lk.22:3-6; Acts 5:3; Lk. 13:10).

Speaking of a person having the character traits of Satan it's one reason why Jesus said, **"FOR YOU ARE THE CHILDREN OF** *your father the devil,* **AND YOU LOVE TO DO THE EVIL THINGS HE DOES...WHEN HE LIES (AND COMMITS OTHER SINS) IT'S CONSISTENT WITH HIS CHARACTER!"** (Jn. 8:44 NLT.) And that's why The writer of Ephesians says, **"We are not**

fighting against people made of flesh and blood, *but against PERSONS WITHOUT BODIES*—of **THE UNSEEN WORLD,** those **mighty SATANIC BEINGS**...*against HUGE NUMBERS OF WICKED SPIRITS IN THE SPIRIT WORLD"* (Eph. 6:12 LBV), *that possess, then have an influence on the way we act, the things we do and say.*

*N*otice in Matthew 8:28 concerning the *"two men who were UNDER THE CONTROL, INFLUENCE OF DEMONS. And when Jesus approached they (the demons living inside the men)* **shrieked** *and* **screamed,** *"Jesus, Son of God, what do want with us? Have you come to punish us before our time?".*

Dear reader, Satan and his demons are similar to *parasites* that take over a person's body and afterwards that person becomes an anthropic host that **supports the demon spirit's existence,** and in turn the **demon reveals itself in the character and personality** of the individual possessed!

When Paul said, **"I DON'T UNDERSTAND MYSELF AT ALL, for I really want to do what is right, but I can't. I do what I don't want to do. I know perfectly well that what I'm doing is wrong... But I can't help myself, BECAUSE I'M NO LONGER DOING IT. There is something else deep within me,** in my lower nature, **THAT IS AT WAR WITH MY MIND..."** (Rom. 7:15-17, 23 LBV), he was referring to "the mighty SATANIC BEINGS and HUGE NUMBERS OF WICKED SPIRITS IN THE SPIRIT

WORLD" that were battling to take control of his reasoning and mentality!

I Was Blind But Now I See

The reason I have been led by the Holy Spirit to point out those verses above is because of a **tiresome, pathetic, lethargic** battle I had with crack cocaine, it counterparts, and the wicked, *possessed* life I was recruited into living by **"the evil spirit of deception"** (Rev.12:9;19:20) **"and rebellion"** (Dt. 1:26,43; Jer.5:23-24).

For years I fought with these *invisible* (Col.1:16) *demonic spirits* of crack cocaine *influence* (see 1Tim.2:14; 2Sam13:3), *suggestion* (Gen. 3:1-4), and *depression* (2Sam.13:20). It was on account of *my lack of knowledge* that I suffered all the heartache, hopelessness, and misery that came along with choosing to ignoring God's word concerning spiritual warfare. Unfortunates such as homelessness, social and family rejection, suicidal thoughts, loss of self-respect, loneliness, just to name a few.

Speaking of *lack of knowledge*, when the writer of Hosea 4:6 stated: **"my people are destroyed for lack of knowledge"**, this *lack of knowledge* or should I say, *"ignorance of the spiritual war we are waged in"* (Rev.12:17) *"against unseen demonic forces that influence us"* that **"suggest disobedience"** (Gen.3:1-6; 1Chr.21:1;Acts5:3;Eph.2:2), **"rebellion and disrespect for the commandments of God's"** (2Kg.7:15; Hos.4:6; 1Sam.12:15; Ezek.2:3-7; Dan.9:5) nearly *destroyed* me, and moreover *"my chances of eternal life in the kingdom of heaven"*. (See Matt.24:37-51; Rom.13:11-14; 1Cor.6:9-10; Rev.21:27; 22; 15).

14

This same *ignorance of Ephesians 6:12* was not only the primary basis behind my lingering addiction, but the reason I tolerated homelessness, perversion, shame and other indignities. Dear reader, before we go any further on the subject of Satan, the chaos he causes in the lives of the innocent, and how to defeat the one called *"the tempter"* (Matt.4:3;1Thess.3:5), I don't want you to get the wrong impression, feel intimidated, start thinking that Satan's some all-powerful being, and that you are powerless. That would be giving him more credit than he deserves over your life. The only dominance that Satan has over you or anyone else is the means of **DECEPTION. It's his only avenue of getting us to sin against God.** (See Gen.2:15-17; 3:1-6, 13-14; Acts 5:3; 1Chr.21:1; 2Chr.32:31).

God is the only immortal being who is *"omnipotent"* (Rev.19:6**)**, possess complete, unlimited, universal power and authority, and "omnipresent" (simultaneously present throughout the whole world, at the same time everywhere).
The eyes of the Lord are in every place, beholding the evil and the good "(Prov.15:3).

"For God's eyes are upon the ways of man, and he sees all..." (Job 34:21 AMP).

Satan Has No Power Aside from Deception

Satan does not have the gift of *omnipotence* or *omnipresence*. He has to rely on a team of those **fallen angels he deceived into joining him in battle against God "** (Rev.12:4, 7-9) as *celestial agents* (1Cor.15:40) to gather information on his victims before planning an attack. According to Revelations 19:20; 20:3, 8, 10; 13:11-14 Satan's only so-called power that he has is the ability to deceive people and evidently angels too. Now that you understand this truth I pray that you no longer continue to walk around feeling intimidated, fearful, or defenseless. The wiser you become in the Word concerning the enemy's tactics, the quicker you'll obtain deliverance and other blessings.

Who Are These Good And Evil Spirits And Where Did They Originate From

Before God fashioned or *"formed man"* (Gen.2:7), **angelic beings existed before** the configuration of man. The Bible confirms, <u>**"before the foundations of the earth were laid (before man was created to roam the earth)...the morning stars sang together, and all the angels shouted for joy"**</u> (Job 38:4, 7). These angelic beings, the first *"sons of God"* (Gen.6:2-4) lived in heaven worshipping at the throne of God. It was only after the fall of man, that *angels, who were already present,* were sent from heaven to guard the tree of life (Gen.3:24).

The Bible testifies that these *earliest living beings,* called *angels* who were on assignment before any human being was ever born or died, that they were *created* first (Ezk.28:13-15; Isa.14:12), and afterwards Adam, Eve, and the rest of the human race (see Gen.4:1-2,16-26;5:1-32;6:1). We are also informed in Scripture of these heavenly beings, their connection with the government of God, and *their relationship concerning the redemption of man* (see Ps.103:19-21; Rev.5:11).

Just as the angels who were sent to guard the tree of life after the fall of man, there are angels who God sends on missions of mercy to the children of God (Heb.1:14). On the other hand there are those angelic spirits who made the choice join Satan in his battle to take over God's throne (Rev.12:4, 7-9), whom we are at spiritual war with (Rev.12:17), and there are other fallen angels that choose not meddle in the business of mankind nor worship God, **"whom God has reserved in everlasting chains under darkness until the judgment of the great day"** (Jude 1:6).

Note that in the beginning Satan and those angels who turn rebellious were created sinless, equal in nature, power, and glory with the holy angels that are God's messengers. But **"fallen through sin"**, these mutinous angelic spirits have joined together for the dishonor of God, and "**the destruction and downfall of human creation"** (Jn.14:30; Rev.12:12b).

Understand That We Share This Planet With Rebellious Angelic Spirits

United with Satan in his revolution (Rev.12:4,7) these *"fallen angels"* cooperate with him in his feud against the peace and happiness of men, and against divine authority: **"Like a great bolt streaking out of the sky, this brilliant angel, shinning with all his glory—glory given to him by God—was cast to the earth. Where did he fall? He fell right where we are, and now we have to deal with him"** (Lk.10:17-18, Forerunner Commentary Bible).

Old testament mentions the existence of these mutinous spirits, howbeit, it was during *"the time of Christ's prophecy"* (Deu.18:15-18;Isa.9:6-7; Mk.1:7-8), *"of which the angels in heaven were the first to get the news"* (Matt.1:20-25;Mk.1:1-2) that Satan began to manifest his powers of negative influence more outstandingly against those who would dare to keep the commandment of God, or live by the teachings of Jesus Christ" (Matt.5:12;Rev.12:17). The Bible tells us that **"our bodies are simply tents"** for our spirits to reside in while here on earth (2Cor.5:1, 4 CEV), and that God, out of love for us also **"prepared a body for his Son, Jesus"** (Heb.10:5; Jn.1:1, 10;

17

Phil.2:6-8) and *sent him down to earth* **"to redeem us"** (Jn.6:38; 1Pet.1:18; Rev.5:9; 14:3).

Christ came to open our eyes, and to reveal the truth to us concerning spiritual warfare (Eph.6:10—12; Rev.12:10b; 18:2). His purpose was specifically to **destroy the works of Satan** (1Jn.3:8; Heb.2:14) by *educating* us (Jn.3:2; 7:28-29; Jn.6:45) on the **presence** and **realism** of **influential, mischief spirits on earth** (Jn.14:30; Eph.2:2; Rev.18:2).

Why Do People Believe Some Text In The Bible But Neglect The Teachings Of Spiritual Warfare

The reason that many people choose to neglect spiritual warfare is because Satan, *"the god of this world ,Satan, has blinded them to the truth"* (2Cor.4:4), by diverting their attention away from the reality of his presence and keeping them occupied with *problems* (Matt.13:18-21), *selfish interests* (Eccl.2:1-11; Rom.13:11-14), and *materialistic* values (Lk.4:5-6; Dan.4:28-30). **As a result they rarely think of evil angels who are constantly seeking access to them** with the intent of influencing addiction, prostitution, homosexuality, tormenting their bodies, and destroying their possessions and lives. No individual is in greater danger from the influence of evil spirits than those who deny the existence and agency of the devil and his angels.

As long as people choose to ignore the *reality and* **"tricks of the devil** (Eph.6:11) and blame their unfortunate circumstances on being in the wrong place at the wrong time…they will forever be taken advantage of by their own ignorance, and overlook God's warning, *"Be on your guard...*

Your enemy, the devil, is like a roaring lion, sneaking around to find someone to attack" (1Pet.5:8 CEV).

The neglect or **IGNORANCE** of Ephesians 6:12**, "the battle that we are waged in against those *rebellious angelic spirits* who manipulate, and control the minds of those who are unconscious of their influence"** (see Eph.2:2) cause me to steal from my family and friends, to sell my furniture, clothing, and other items, to neglect my spouse, children and their needs, to disregard paying rent and other utilities, which ultimately led to 20 years of drug abuse, homelessness, countless drug rehabilitation center visits, and of course prison time. **I Became The Modern Day Prodigal Son Reduced To Homelessness And Eating Out Of The Trash**

Traveling across the country I slept many a cold nights underneath suspension viaducts, in the woods, the local Park, old abandoned houses and cars, in condemned buildings, beneath railway bridges, in public restrooms on the urine stained floors, underneath the crawl space of empty homes, holes in the ground I dug with a stick and covered myself with leaves to keep warm, and anywhere else I could find a place to rest. And many a night I'd wearily stagger the city streets until the next day.

Whenever I'd arrive in a new county or State I survive by locating the nearest Homeless Shelter, Rescue Mission, or Salvation Army residence where I stood in line for a bed for the night, food, clothing, and other handouts. On the days when I got kicked out of those places for not passing a breathalyzer, not making it back before curfew, or some other drug addicted reason, I'd go to different restaurants wait for a customer to approach the trash can and pathetically say to them, *"Excuse me, do you mind if I get those scraps off of your plate before you throw then in the trash. I noticed that you left a good little bit of meat on some of the bones. I'm sorry to bother you, but I'm starving."*

When things really got rough I stole from convenient and grocery stores; out of the refrigerator of the hospital nurses station, from the cupboards or refrigerator of whoever would allow me into their home; scavenged through restaurant dumpsters and garbage cans, from apple trees and grape vines, or picked through the decomposed, rotten vegetables and fruits that were thrown out at the end of the day by local produce merchants. And when it came to hygiene a goat would have been more pleasant to be around. I had become a modern day real life *"prodigal son":*

"There was a certain man who had two sons; And the younger of them said to his father, Father, give me the part of the property that falls [to me]. And he divided the estate between them. And not many days after that, the younger son gathered up all that he had and journeyed into a distant country, and there he wasted his fortune in reckless, wild and loose [from restraint] living.

And when he had spent all he had, a mighty famine came upon that country, and he began to fall behind and be in want. So he went and forced (glued) himself upon one of the citizens of that country, who sent him into his fields to feed hogs. And he would gladly have fed on and filled his belly with the carob pods (hog SLOP) that the hogs were eating, but [they could not satisfy his hunger and] **nobody gave him anything [better].** <u>**Then when he came to himself,**</u> he said, How many hired servants of my father have enough food, and [even food] to spare, but I am perishing (dying) here of hunger!"** (Lk.15:11-17 AMP).

20

My friend, **IT'S TIME FOR YOU ALSO, TO** *"come to yourself!"* let the crack pipe go, get off the streets, off the prostitution corner, and like the prodigal son **"Go Back to Your heavenly Father"** (LK.15:18), admit your sin, that *you need* his help, and He will likewise say to you, **"My son/daughter was lost, but now he's found"** (vs. 24).

I Truly Wanted To Live For God But...

I must admit that I tried desperately to quit numerous times but the results didn't last long. I went in and out of countless rehabs, joined N.A., A.A. support groups, had a sponsor, signed myself into a clinic for the depressed, went to church, had folk pour anointing oil and lay hands on me, and finally I was fortunate enough to become part of A Bible Training Center For The Drug Addicted, where I excelled to several leadership positions during my two and a half year obligation. Things were looking fairly well for me until somewhere along my second year I decided that I was strong enough to move off campus and manage on my own. The neighborhood I moved into was somewhat drug infested, though not as awful or corrupt as the area God had formerly delivered me out of, but nevertheless drug activity was visible.

Well, six months after moving out on my own, trying to be a genuine witness by going into the crack houses, back allies and hideouts to minister to struggling addicts, without warning ill fortune struck again. It seemed that no matter how sincere I was to live for God somehow I ended up returning to the miserable, homeless, wretched, crack addicted life style.

What Was Happening To Me Lord

My life reflected that of the Apostle Paul when he was having problems staying on the right path and stated:

"I don't understand what I do. I don't do what I want to do. Instead, I do what I hate to do...As it is, I'm no longer the one who does these things. IT'S SIN LIVING IN ME. I know there's nothing good in my sinful nature. I want to do what's good, but I can't. I don't do the good things I want to do. I KEEP ON DOING THE EVIL THINGS I DON'T WANT TO DO...But I'm not really the one who is doing it. Its sin in me...Deep inside I find joy in God's law (I want to please God by how I live).

But I see another law working in parts of my body. It fights against the law of my mind...So in my mind I'm a slave to God's law (I want to please Him). But in my sinful nature I'm a slave to... sin" (Rom.7:15, 17-20, 22-23, 25 NIV).

Can you relate to Paul's declaration of guilt? My friend, **"the war that his *sinful nature* was waging against his *spiritual nature,* or his desire to do what he knew was right"** (see Gal. 5:17) was a battle against demonic, *unseen angelic spirits* (2Kg.6:17) that suggest rebellion. Paul is simply trying to tell us that it's not you or I who fall victim to drug addiction, alcoholism, prostitution, whoredom, homosexuality, or perversion. It's not you or I that becomes bitter, angry, quarrelsome, hateful, jealous, prejudice or contemptuous. It's not you or I who utter curse words, steal, lie, cheat, get involved in gossip or acts of hypocrisy. It's not you or I that entertain thoughts of revenge, murder, or rape.

According to the Word of God it is our battle **"AGAINST PERSONS WITHOUT BODIES—the evil rulers of THE UNSEEN WORLD, THOSE SATANIC BEINGS... and against huge numbers of WICKED SPIRITS IN THE SPIRIT World** *that influence* the way we react to the **confrontations, "tests"** (Job 23:10:7:18), and **"trials"** (1Pet.1: 7), of this life.

I KNOW WHAT I'M DOING IS WRONG BUT I CAN'T HELP MYSELF

According to Romans 7:15-25, the Apostle Paul came to understand this spiritual phenomenon and the reason behind his own shortcomings when he said: **"I know perfectly well what I'm doing is wrong...**but I can't help myself, **BECAUSE I'M NO LONGER DOING IT. Its sin inside of me that's stronger than I am that makes me do these evil things"** (Rom.7: 16-17 LBV).

My friend, as Paul, we must all come to the realization that the reason we have so many up's and down's in our spiritual walk is because **"we are engaged in a war against the invisible influences of evil, wicked spirits in the spirit world" (Eph.6:12), "which** *possess,* **take over a person's body, mind, thereby** instigating sin. (See Eph.2:2; Matt.4:24; 8:28; Lk.7:21; Acts19:12, 13). Paul again confirms in one of his sermons that **we are indeed in a spiritual conflict against evil forces** when he preached about **"the spirit world with its kings and kingdoms, its rulers and authorities"** (Col.1: 16b LBV).

23

When Paul spoke about "the spirit world with its kings, kingdom's, ruler's and authorities", Paul was simply trying to inform the church, *and us* about another sphere of activity, a spirit world, which humans cannot see, nevertheless being organized under the same bureaucratic principles as our earth world is. Just as our world have a president, governor, senators, as well as different positions of authority. The spirit world according to Colossians 1:16 also have its king's...rulers and authorities. Our world has a military ARMY with its Majors, Generals, Sergeants and privates; the spirit world also has a military ARMY with different positions of authority and rank as is evident in 2kings 6:15-17;Matthew 24: 31 and Revelations 12:7.

In the book of Daniel there is evidence of this *organized* world of spiritual forces in the heavenly realms. Notice that when Daniel was praying to God, that the devil heard Daniels prayer and immediately sent out demon angels to delay the answer: God said to Daniel, **"Don't be afraid...I have come to give you an answer"** (Dan.10:12). And when Daniel finally understood what was causing the delay, he responded: **"But the prince of Persia (Satan and his demonic forces being in control of the surrounding circumstances) opposed me for 21 days. Then Michael (God's chief angel) came to help me..."** (Dan.10:13 NIV).Yes, God's Word truly verifies that there are indeed, *"evil forces and authorities... in the spirit world* organized by Satan, who is constantly devising a plan for the downfall of mankind ever since he was defeated in his attempted to overtake God's throne according to Revelations 12:9, 12-17, Isaiah 14:13, and Ezekiel 28:17.

24

2

CAN PEOPLE REALLY BE POSSESSED BY DEMONS

*T*he reason that the Church and society remains ignorant of spiritual warfare and the probability of **can a person actually be possessed by an evil spirit and influence or made to rebel against the commandments of God** is because most of them haven't been taught first of all most individuals have a fraction of pride that won't let them consider the possibility and truth of God's word concerning demonic possession, and would rather accept hear sermon about prosperity, blessings, healing, deliverance, and going to heaven. The Bible defines preachers who *cater,* teach to such a congregation as *Pastors "preaching to itching ears"* (2Tim.4:3), which simply means they teach on and tell the congregation exactly what they'd rather hear instead of the truth.

"**For the time is coming when [people] will not tolerate (endure) sound and wholesome instruction, but, having ears itching [for something pleasing and gratifying], they will gather to themselves one teacher after another to a considerable number, chosen to satisfy their own liking and to foster the errors they hold**" (amplified version).

The second and third reasons are that the Church has not been explicitly taught *"who they are"*, as *"threefold" beings,* "body, soul, and spirit" (1Thess. 5:23; 1Jn.5:7-8; 1Cor.5:5; Job 7:11), and most importantly **"how man *first* being created in God's image and likeness"** (Gen.1:26-27) *is receptive to being possessed by celestial influences of evil or filled by the good characteristic of God's Holy Spirit.*

Because Man Is A Threefold Essence He's Open To Being Possessed Or Filled

The significant difference between being **"POSSESSED"** by the *rebellious* spirit and characteristics of Satan and his demons (see Matt.4:24; 8:16, 28; 9:32; 12:22,43-45), and being guided, **"FILLED"**, with the presence of God's *Holy Spirit* (see Lk.1:15; Eph.5:18;Phil.1:11; Acts 4:8; 9:17) is that a demon spirits will forcefully, without being invited or any regard make you his property, **POSSESSION,** *posse* you. Similar to the way the old heartless, excruciating, tempered negro salve owners who would carefully examine their potential slaves by forcefully looking into the mouths and other areas of interest like they did horses before buying, *possessing,* claiming them as their property.

For example after a horse was bought the one who **possessed** the claim then took it home, placed the animal into a stall, occasionally feed it hay and afterwards use it to perform unsympathetic, degrading tasks without any real regard for the animal, which they had possessed, bought as property. Well, the devil, like the slave owner also first will carefully examine his potential victims by looking into their lives for areas of *willful sins* that would allow his

26

passage to enter. And if he's satisfied he will make an attempt to *possess*, the property (the body of the person), and like the heartless slave owner uses the person to perform, act out, or voice his anger and bitterness towards God. Satan, like the salve owner will also take that which he has possessed, purchased home, or should I say *make the person his home* (Lk.11:24) and from time to time feeds his possession not hay but crack cocaine, alcohol, or some other drug to keep them under his control and influence.

Another example of being **POSSESSED** is similar to how an abusive, heartless, forceful husband treats his fragile wife. Instead of treating her as a loving child of God's he shows her no respect, as if she's simply something to be *possessed, his property, to be slapped around, taken advantage of, used and abused. He* sees her as simply his possession. Someone he can control by fear and deception to be molded into his personal slave. She becomes "a shell of a person" with no real say so in the relationship. She is only to do as she's told, as she is forcibly instructed to do. The devil's primary intention, or his purpose for wanting to *"possess"* a person is to steer them down the path of sin and rebellion (Eph.2:2), to *alienate* them from a life of God (Eph.4:17-18;1Cor.6:9-10; Jn.10:10), to get into their hearts and cause them to betray Jesus, the Word (Lk.22:3; Jn.13:2), thereby disregarding the commandments of God (Acts 5:3; 1Chr.21:1).

On the other hand the to be **FILLED** with the benevolent, gentle, caring, reverential presence of God's Holy Spirit, the Spirit that promotes reverence and respect for God's Word their life will be totally different. When one is *filled* with God's Holy Spirit the person they are given a certain measure of power and authority from God *to* **"live a righteous life"** here on earth (see

27

Lk.1:15;Jn.14:14-17,26;15:26; Eph.2:1-5;Gal.5:22-25), how to *"witness"* (Acts 1:2,5,8; 15:8; Jn.1:7; 1Jn.1:5; 5:6 Acts 2:2-4;4:8), *"to become an instrument"* for God's purpose (Isa. 9:6-7; 11:1-10; Lk.1:31-32; Acts 19:6; 28:8; Lk.13:3; Mk.16:17-18). If we choose to *invite* God's Holy Spirit he will change our lives for the better, *"give us wisdom and direction"* (Acts11:12; 16:6-7; 15:28), *"joy, peace, and the power to live a victorious life here on earth"* (Eph.6:11-19).

The Holy Spirit Does Not What To Forcefully Possess Or Dominate You

God, the Holy Spirit does not what to forcefully possess or dominate us in any way. He will not, without a cheerful, welcomed invitation invade your space or body. God, the Holy Spirit will not aggressively *force* himself on us because he'd rather we show him that we love him by the way we live. God respectfully, as he did with Christ, gives us the *"choice"* to serve Him,(see Isa. 7:15-16; Josh.24:15;1Kg.18:21;Prov.1:29), to personally welcome, invite His Holy Spirit to come in either by *"asking in prayer"* (Lk.11:11-13;Matt.7:7-11; Zech.12:10;Joel 2:23,28), or by God through a Pastor or Christian who has been ordained to *"lay hands"* (Acts 8:17-22;19:6;Dt.34:9).

The entity of God's Holy Spirit is one of his greatest gifts to man. His main function is to help us to enjoy a favorable life, to strengthen us when we're weak, to comfort us during times of sorrow, and even to *put the right words in our mouths as we pray to God* (Rom.8:26-27). *"As sure as there is a physical body, there is a spiritual body"* (1Cor.15:44). One of a "Holy" nature that promotes Christian character and reverence for God (Rom. 8:1-16; Gal.5:16-17,22-25), and one of a *"rebellious"* nature and character that suggest sin and rebellion towards God (Eph. 2:2;Rev.12:4,7-9).

The Battle Is Over Your Soul And Eternal Life

My Friend, Luke 16: 19-31 proves that the spiritual war that you in is a battle is for your soul! The text specifically points out the fact *that the unsaved and lost are in hell.* They are *conscious* and possess full use of their faculties such as being able to see, hear, feel smell, and remember their life on earth (v.25), but unfortunately they are in torment (Rev.14:11). The passage also indicates that hell is not just a place that sinners will spend eternity, but the state and condition of the departed human *spirit* after death (Matt.25:31-34, 41,46). I realize now why the writer **"spake of the resurrection of Christ, that his soul was not left in hell"** (Acts 2:31, 27). I pray that your soul will also not be left in hell!

Now that you understand the difference between the two entities my question is to you, "would you prefer to be *possessed* or *filled?* For an up close and more personal experience from real people, with real testimonies who temporarily died and either went to heaven or hell I urgently suggest you get the DVD entitle, *"Life Beyond The Grave"* by Pat Robertson of the 700 Club, and the book, *"Divine Revelation Of Hell"*, by Mary K. Baxster.

The first thing that inquiring minds need to grasp is that **GOD FIRST CREATED ADAM AS A SPIRIT BEING,** in His very own *image* and *likeness.* And since God's image is of a spirit nature (Jn.4:24), then there's no doubt that His *first* representation of Adam was that of a spirit form. Notice carefully that God didn't **"form a body"** for

29

Adam and *"breath Adam's spirit into that bodily form"* until after He completed the Garden of Eden (see Genesis 2:7-8). Just as God is a spirit, Adam was also a spirit being until he took on human form which then made him a human being. And likewise you are **a spirit being, with a soul, simply living inside a constructed human body while here living on earth** (1Thess. 5:25).

Notice that Christ also appreciate and *"praised God for his own human constructed body"* (see Heb.10:5; Jn.1:1014) to inhabit in while he was on earth.

Well, demons are spirits without human bodies (but desperately searching for one to inhabit in order to express themselves in this world. They long to find expression but can't until they're in *possession* a body:

"But when the unclean spirit has gone out of a man (a demon spirit has been cast out), it roams through dry [arid] places in search of rest, but it does not find any. Then it says, "I will go back to my house from which I came out." And when it arrives, it finds the place unoccupied, swept, put in order, and decorated. Then it goes and brings with it seven other spirits more wicked than itself, and they go in and make their home there. And the last condition of that man becomes worse than the first. So also shall it be with this wicked generation" (Matt.12:43-45 AMP)

What Actually Is An Unclean Spirit

Let me break down the above verse so you will have a better understanding of what an unclean spirit is and what Christ is saying. The very first sentence tells you right off the bat that you're dealing with a demonic spirit who has been cast out of someone. The verse says—"When an unclean spirit goes out of a man." An *unclean spirit* is **a demonic spirit and** *The fact that it is going out of the man means the demon was indeed on the inside of the man!* And if the demon is going out of the man, then he had to either be cast out of him by another Christian or direct by God Himself. Otherwise, the demon would have never left the man on his own accord. Once a demon is able to get on the inside of someone, they will not leave unless they are either cast out by God or another Christian acting under God's leading and authority to cast the demon out.

The next sentence says that "the demon then wants to return to the house" from which he came out of earlier. The house he is referring to was the person's body that he was cast out of earlier. After a demon is cast out, this verse tells us that *the same demon will then periodically* return *to see if the person has slipped up* in any way in order to give him the legal right to be able to enter back into him again. Demons cannot enter into a person's body just because they want to. There are spiritual laws that are in operation in the spirit realm and demons have to abide by these laws set up by God. In order for a demon to be able to enter in a person's body, they have to have some kind of legal right, or *legal permission* to be able to do so as is noted in Job 1:6-12.

In the case of having a legal right to the person's body the person has to *ignorantly engage into some type of sin* that only then gives the demon the legal right to be able to

31

enter into them. Common door openers that will allow demons to come in on you are *drugs,* abusing alcohol, fornication, adultery, homosexuality, any type of occult activity such as witchcraft, and of course Satan worship. That's why people take a very big gamble every time they engage in any of the above activities. And once a demon moves in, take over the person's body that individual is going to be in big trouble! That's when then the demons will have to either be cast out of the person by God Himself or by God through another anointed Christian. The demons will not voluntarily give up their position once they are inside of a person's body. Also notice in the verse that once the demon is cast out he is seeking rest and finds none. This verse tells you right there that demons would prefer to be living on the inside of a person's body rather than roaming through the air. This is why most of them will put up some kind of fight once an actual deliverance starts up. Once The Demon Returns

The next sentence is the key. **Once the demon returns, goes back** to the same person he had originally lived in, *he will check him out to see if he has any legal right to be able to enter back into him.* The demon will look for *signs of drug usage, sexual immorality, cursing, hatred, bitterness, anger, jealousy, prejudice, or some other sin.* If the demon finds *the house empty* (a person's body, heart void from living a life that's pleasing to God) he then apparently has the legal right to be able to enter back into that person. The fact that God is using the word *"empty"* to let us know that people who have demons cast out must become *Spirit-filled* in order to keep the demons from returning! In other words they have to receive the baptism of the Holy Spirit, and then learn to *"walk in the spirit"* (see Gal.5:16-25) so that when the demon does try to return he will not find the person's house (their mind, heart) *"empty"*, but *"filled"* with the presence of the Holy Spirit.

My friend, after a demon is *cast out* God expects you to start walking and growing in Him, the Word. **God wants that empty space to be filled up with His knowledge, presence and grace – and the only way that can happen is if you start growing and maturing in the Lord.** That's why it's so important that you immediately find yourself a church home and begin to grow surrounded by the protecting family of God!

Start Feeding Your Soul (Mind) With God's Word

Once the demon enters into the person's body, they will then enter into the person's **soul.** If this person is a Christian, the demon cannot enter into the person's spirit because the Holy Spirit is already residing there. But *if the person's soul has not been baptized and filled with the Holy Spirit,* the demon can then enter into the person's *soul (mind)* as well as his body. This is why it's imperative that the person become Spirit-filled after a deliverance so as to prevent this from ever happening again. When you receive the baptism of the Holy Spirit, He will then be able speak to you through your thoughts thereby giving you a measure of self-control so that the demon will no longer be able to overpower that your soul (mind) again. This attribute of **"self-control"** is *a gift, fruit of the Holy Spirit* that you have to *"pray for"* (see Gal.5:22-24; Lk.11:9-13; 1Cor.12:1, 4-11) so that you won't give in so easily to your flesh, or the thoughts of the devil.

"For those who are according to the flesh and are **controlled** *by its unholy desires set their minds on and*

33

pursue those things which gratify the flesh, but those who are according to the **Spirit and are controlled** by the desires of the Spirit set their minds on and seek those things which gratify the [Holy] Spirit. **Now the mind of the flesh [which is sense and reason without the Holy Spirit]** is death [death that comprises all the miseries arising from sin, both here and hereafter]. But the mind of the [Holy] Spirit is life and [soul] peace [both now and forever].

Now as we move further into analyzing Matthew 12:43-45 the verse also tells us that **if the demon finds the house empty and *"not in order,"* not only will he enter back in, but he is going to be bringing back with him 7 more demon spirits** that are going to be even wicked than he is! This one verse is thus telling you that there are *levels of evil* even among demons themselves. In other words, some demons are going to be meaner and more evil than others. Each demon will have his own assignment *associated with its name* (see Mk.9:29). The demon's name will tell you what its functions were on the inside of that person's body and soul. And as they are coming out "one by one" during the person's deliverance, the demonized person will then begin to finally understand where all of those negative emotions were coming from in the first place. This is why the Bible says that the truth will set you free!

A Demon Spirit Is Simply An Entity Personality

A demon is SIMPLY a personality—a spirit being, just like you and me. The only difference is that God constructed a *primal,* human body for our spirits to reside in while living here on earth (Gen.2:7). However, envious demon spirits (Dt.7:7), *entities* without bodies with which to express themselves in this world long to find

34

expression but can't until they're in possession of a body according to Matthew 12:43-45. **A Demon Is A Personality**—an entity, a spirit being, just like Adam, you and I were in the beginning. The only difference is that God constructed a *primal, human body* to transfer our entity forms or spirits into in order that we would be able to exist here on earth (Gen.2:7; Eccl. 12:7). In simple terms a Spirit is basically what's known as an *"entity"*. The Webster Dictionary describes an entity as "a spirit being, a life form, a being existence which is independent, separate, self-contained with its own identification and characteristics that are associated with its personality. **A disembodied spirit being"**.

My friend, as we yearn to do good, live right, respect God's moral code of living according to the His Written Word, to express ourselves in conversation, as we respond to certain impulses, urges or desires, **demon spirits hunger to express themselves!** But since they have no *human body* of their own they must wander the earth (see Matt.12:43-45) seeking a body in which they can enter and use to express themselves by carrying out their missions of "evil influence" according to Lk.22:3, Acts 5:1-9, 1Chr.21:1 and Gen.3:1. **We can best understand who Satan is by the names given to him in the Bible.** The word devil merely means *"spiritual enemy of God's and man's"* (Matt. 13:39; Lk.10:19; Acts 13:10), *"a wicked spirit"* (Matt.13:19, 38), *"deceiver of mankind"* (1Tim.2:14; Rev, 19:20; 20:10), and *"accuser"* (Rev.12:10).

Since *a human body has the broadest* means of expression, and because the human body is the only one made in the likeness of God, demons, rebellious spirits consider it as their highest prize to enter human beings and encourage immorality. The fact is that *a person can either be influenced by God's moral Spirit* (Gen.41:38; Num.24:2), or *the power of Satan's immoral spirit* (Acts 26:18; Matt.4:24; 8:16, 28; 12:22). If more Pastor's and leaders of the church would teach on this subject more than they actually do then society as a whole would not be so reluctant to accept and understand God's teaching on spiritual warfare. And because they don't people are left ignorant to form their own opinions about the reasons that they or their friends commit the sins and abominations they do. *Such as the sin of fornication, adultery, homosexuality, cursing, stealing, murder, drug and alcohol abuse, and much more.* For those reasons the Bible tells us that we should **"test each spirit to see if it comes from God or not"** (1Jn.4:1 NIV).

When it comes to the question, *"how can I tell the difference between a person, like the apostle Paul, who was **wrestling with sin**, wanting to do right but found it difficult (see Rom.7:9-25), and a person **who is possessed** by an evil spirit and doesn't think twice repenting?"* (See Ps.36:1-4) the answer is that first of all, not all unbelievers are demonized. The truth of the matter is that both the unbeliever and the believer "**contend**" with carnal, fleshly desires. The only difference is that **"the believer will not keep on sinning"**, *or* "**continue to give in to the influence of sin**" once the Spirit of God truly takes over (1Jn.3:6 CEV).

It's only after the sin becomes **habituated, the habit or sin becomes a lifestyle that demonic influence take root.** Plainly put, "you can recognize a person who

36

has encountered an evil spirit by their **"habitual sinful conduct"** and lifestyle. Such as *habitual* cursing, drug usage; choosing to disregard sexual sins like fornication, adultery, and homosexuality which falls under the category of **"willfully sinning"** (Heb.10:26), or **"not being sorry for the sin"** to the point of where the sorrow causes you to *stop the persistence* (see Ps.38:17-18).

The Scofield Study Bible footnotes points out one sign of a demon possessing a person commenting on Matthew 13:30 by stating, " ***The first sign that a person has encountered a demonic spirit is when that person stops or has no real desire to attend church and fellowship on a regular basis"***, when the Bible sternly tells us, **"Not to forsake the assembling of ourselves together, as the manner of some is..."** (Heb.10:25).

Now you might try to justify yourself by saying, "I just stop for a while to gather myself", "I don't like where I'm going to church and I'm looking for another", "I watch religious services on television regularly", or some other reason, but the fact is that if you have stopped or lost the drive and desire to attend, fellowship on a regular basis you most likely have encountered a demonic spirit that, by the way, has no desire for church *because the deception of Satan is so intense that they can't perceive the wrong in their lives and want to change"*.

Specifically speaking when it comes to the *drug addict, "fornicator, adulterer, homosexual, thief, greedy person, drunkard, or anyone who curses"* (1Cor.6:9-10 CEV) they simply "... **have no fear of God to restrain them. In their BLIND CONCEIT they can't see how wicked they really**

37

are...and therefore they make no attempt to turn from the evil" (Ps.36:1-4 NLB).

Those illustrations above are just a few signs to look for that indicates that a person most likely has encountered or is being influenced by an evil spirit.

For As Many As Are Led By The Spirit Of God They Are The Sons Of God.

On the other **hand a PERSON WHO IS SINCERE about being or becoming a follower of Christ will show UNWAVERING, CONSISTENT signs of being under the *influence* of the Holy Spirit.** There should be signs of a **"daily dying"** to sin (1Cor.15:31) as one surrenders to His *leading, guidance,* and process of being *transformed.* (See Rom.12:2; 6:6; 2Cor.5:17; Eph.4:22; Col.3:9). The Holy Spirit's *influence* will grow into everlasting devoutness, peace, and harmony, and **"If our minds are ruled by the Spirit we will have life and peace"** (Rom.8:6b CEV).

When a person's mind is under the *influence* and *guidance* of God's Holy Spirit they will take heed to the *"something told me not to do that, say that, or go there"* little voice inside of them. One example of paying attention to the Holy Spirit's leading or influence can be found in Acts 21:4 where Paul gave heed to the Spirit's leading when *something told him* "not to go the Jerusalem because trouble awaited." For other examples of the Spirit's leading read Acts 8:29; 10:19; 11:12 and 16:7.

38

As you examine the Gospels you will notice that the teaching and subject of demonic *possession* was one of Jesus' main topics. I want you to also notice that the first clue we get concerning Satan's need for a body is where he took **possession** of the snakes body in order to approach and entice Eve into sinning. (See Genesis 3:1-5). For that reason, in today's society when it comes to healing or deliverance it is a must that you comprehend this preternatural occurrence.

The first thing I want you to understand is that *just as the righteous* "Spirit of God operates in the hearts of those who *do right* (Gal.5:16,22-25;Rom.8:9-1;Acts 2:41), that "the rebellious spirit of Satan Is at work in the hearts of those who refuse to obey God". (See Eph. 2:2; Acts 5:3; Gal.5:19-21).

Yes Demon Spirits Truly Have The Ability To Speak Through People

Beginning with Matthew 8:28-32, we find two men *"possessed with devils"* who lived in the cemetery. These demon spirits—operating undetected by the natural eye inside the man's body—recognized Jesus and spoke through one of the men, saying, *"Jesus, Son of God, what do you want with us? Have you come to punish us before our time?"*

This is only one example in the Bible that confirms that they *do exist;* they *can possess* a body, and *communicate verbally* through certain individuals. I want you to pay close attention to the fact that they specifically addressed

Jesus as the *Son of God.* Proving that they recognized Jesus as the Son of God, they were aware of His purpose for coming down to earth, and knew they'd eventually be *punished* for their rebellion against God (Matt.8: 29). For Satan and his cohorts to know all this about Jesus, it is evidence that at one time—before being evicted into the atmosphere of earth—they lived in heaven and served at the throne of God (see Rev.4: 8-11; 5:2; 9:19; 12:7). As we take a closer examination of Matt.8: 29 I want you to notice that the Bible says, **"They"** (the demons) **"cried out..."**

The reason I pointed that out is to help you realize that demons undeniably have the ability to cry out, *verbalize* themselves through people. That being said, whenever you hear someone *cursing* or *acting out* in a *fit* of rage, remember **it's really not that person speaking or acting out,** but the character of the demon spirit voicing himself. If you could keep in mind that **"A Demon Is Simply A Rebellious Spirit Personality"** (see Eph.6:12; Rev.12:7-9.17) acting out or expressing his anger towards righteousness it would be easier for you to fight the influence.

To shed more light on a person being influence by a demon spirit personality, let's not forget about *"the man who lived in the graveyard and wandered in the hills...screaming and cutting himself with sharp pieces of stone. But when he saw Jesus and had run to meet him, and fell down before him...* **JESUS SPOKE TO THE DEMON** Acting out **WITHIN THE MAN** *and said, "Come out, you evil spirit"* (Mk.5: 3, 5-7 LBV).

Notice That Jesus Addressed The Demon   **Not The Individual Person**

What I'm trying to get you to understand is that **Jesus spoke to the demon that had *possessed* the man,** not directly to that man. Just as the man was overtaken by insanity, many people today don't realize that the insane, unholy things they say and do is because they too are being controlled by a **demonic spirit within them** as well. The verse clearly indicates the activity of demonic spirits taking over a person's mentality, causing them to say and do that which they know is contrary to the Word of God.

You're Hosting More Than One Demon Spirit

In another account of demonic possession the Bible speaks of *"a slave girl* **who had an evil spirit** *that enabled her to predict the future"* (Acts 16:16.) Elsewhere, the word of God acknowledges "some women who had been healed of evil **spirits...** *And Mary (who was called Magdalene)*, **FROM WHOM SEVEN DEMONS HAD BEEN DRIVEN OUT** (Lk.8: 2).

Isn't it shocking that one individual could house seven or more demonic spirits! Well, what about the man who was *"possessed with a legion"* of demons, 1000 or more (Mk.5: 9). Well, that being said, if you've ever question the reason that you backslide or battles with sin it may be because you too are wrestling with "more than one" evil influence. If so, you need to identify and rebuke them!

Notice carefully in Mk.5: 9-11 that the man—or to be precise, *the demons speaking through the man*—begged **Jesus not to send them to some distant land, but to send them into the nearby pigs.** It doesn't matter if it's by

41

interaction with humans or animal, demon spirits must have a body to operate in to carry out their mayhem in the earth.

Demons Always Make An Attempt To Return To Their Former Host So Stand Strong

The book of Matthew supports this fact by stating, **"This evil nation is like a man possessed by a demon. For if the demon leaves, it goes into the desert for a while (wanders around the city) for a while, seeking rest but finding none. THEN IT SAYS, I WILL RETURN TO THE MAN I CAME FROM..."** (Matt.12: 43 NIV).

The assertion, *"I will return to the man I came from"* indicates that demons do have the ability to *possess* or take over a person's body and mind. Before ending this chapter I want you to clearly understand that according to Luke 9:1 and Mark 16:17 **you have authority over these evil uninvited quests** that attempt to *possess* your body and therefore I pray that you don't fall into a environmental condition of fear when it come s to putting a stop to their influence!

To do so would be to give Satan too much honor and ownership of your body which does not belong to him! And when the devil is given more than his due it allows him to feed on our fears and as a result it intensifies our insecurities. *Your body rightfully belongs to the Holy Spirit of God* (1Cor.6:19), and **"demon possession simply implies a _"limited"_ influence over one or more areas of a person's life."**

42

Just as those devils had *no authority* over the bodies of the men, but begged Jesus to let them *possess* the pigs" (Mk.5:10-12), they much less have any authority over people made in the image of God. We need therefore to fear God alone *"to whom the earth belongs, the world, and all its inhabitants"* (Ps.24:1). Everyday boldly tell the devil: "The word of God lets me know that my body belongs to the Holy Spirit. So by the cleansing power of **the blood of Jesus,** and in **the name of Jesus** I command all uninvited, unholy spirits to depart from my body and make room for the Holy Spirit! Amen."

3

WHY AM I HOOKED

ON CRACK LORD

While I was on my knees pleading for God's help and direction, suddenly, I perceived "the voice of the Lord", and He said to me: "My son, the reason that you are having so much chaos and confusion in your life is because you are not aware of the SPIRITUAL war that you are in or who your opponent truly is."

You Need To Know Who Your Struggle Is Really Against

The voice of the Lord continued, "You have not become conscious of who your opponent really is or the corrupt "powers of darkness and spiritual forces of evil" (Eph. 6:12 NIV) that operate in the sphere of your world. Your opponent is none other than Satan! He once went by the name Lucifer. He was my "chief angel" (see Isa.14:12), appointed overseer of heavens province.

He was more "clever" (Gen.3:1), stunning, and decorative than any of the other angels in heaven (Ezk.28:13). However, out of pride (Ezk.28:17a) he attempted to exalt himself above Me in an unsuccessful effort to take over my throne (Isa. 14:13-15). He waged a war in heaven (Rev.12:7), which ultimately led to his defeat and ejection (Rev.12:8), along with "one third" of the angels of heaven, of whom he was able to deceive into joining him in contention against Me" (Rev.12: 4).

UNDECTED BY THE NATURAL EYE MAN CAN NOT UNDERSTAND THE EVIL FORCES AT WORK IN THE ATMOSPHERE

"These rebellious spirits, along with Satan were cast into the earth's realm (see Rev.12:9), and there they still abide. Undetected by *natural instincts* or the human eye (see Col.1: 16), man cannot see these spiritual forces at work in the atmosphere. Nevertheless they are there. (See 2Kgs.6:15-17). As long as the human race continues to ignore this truth, and to view life only from the *"natural"* (see 1Cor.2: 14), man will remain a victim of circumstance".

Continuing God said, "Essentially because Satan was stripped of his position as the anointed cherub (Ezek.28:14), defeated and expelled from My presence *into the atmosphere of earth* (Rev.12:8-9) he has vowed to continue a wage of war *"against the Word"* (Mk.4:17), and *"all those who would dare to keep My commandments and confess that they belong to Jesus"* (see Rev.12:13, 17 LBV).

When You Backslid You Open Doors To Satanic Attack

"Once you also prepared to dedicate yourself unto Me, but unfortunately went astray. And when you did, you exposed yourself to a multitude of demon spirits. They being

45

more wicked than the first one you encountered, and were delivered from. When a demon is cast out of a man, it goes to the deserts, searching there for rest; but finding none, it returns to the person it left... <u>THEN IT GOES AND GETS SEVEN OTHER DEMONS MORE EVIL THAN</u>

<u>ITSELF</u>, and they enter the man, AND SO THE POOR FELLOW IS SEVEN TIMES WORST OFF THAN HE WAS BEFORE (Lk.11: 24-26 LBV).

You're Now Fighting Against More Than One Demon Spirit

Ongoing God said, "That is why you are having such a hard time getting off drugs...and rededicating your life back to Me", the Lord said. "You are fighting against more than one demon now! What you have to do now is learn to recognize these sinful spirits; learn how to *"bind"* (Matt.12:28-29; 16:19 Mk.3:27), and *"rebuke"* (Lk.4:33; 35, 39-41), these uninvited quests out by their INDIVIDUAL names. Speaking of *demon spirits* having individual names, just as My Son Christ had to address the "deaf and dumb spirit" (Mk.9:17) that possessed the boy; reprimanded the spirit that possessed a man which caused him to have epileptic seizures (Lk.9:39), then REBUKE the demon spirit by its individual name, you must follow his example if you wish to be free of those rebellious spirits that possess and persuade you into using or committing other *sins*".

Once an Addict Always an Addict Is the Devil's Lie

46

I remained kneeling at the door of the as the perception of God's voice persistent: "*Starting today I want you to rededicate yourself to Me. I will reveal to you the road to deliverance, and you will disclose that road to others struggling with drugs, alcohol, and other sins. For I have observed from heaven many who are struggling to be free, yet have been led to believe—according to man's reasoning and psychological counseling—that once they are addicted, they will always be addicted, and that they will never truly be free*".

" *I, the God who created you, the God who sent his only begotten Son into the world, with your deliverance in mind (see Jn.10: 10, LBV) rebuke the devil's lie and say unto you, "If My Son therefore shall make you free, ye shall be free indeed" (Jn.8: 36)*". God concluded, "*Does not My Word declare that Jesus, my Son, is a healer of "divers" (a variety of) diseases and sicknesses? (See Lk.4: 40-41). Well, if he cured those people of their addictions, depressions, and illnesses, then why is it so hard for your generation to believe and understand that he's still the same, "Jesus Christ...yesterday today and forever?"* (Heb.13: 8, NIV).

Why Do Most Crack Addicts Relapse Soon After They're Released from Rehabs or Prisons

Although there are countless drug rehabilitation centers across the land and circuit judges are ordering drug addicts to attend counseling as part of their prison sentencing their recovery only last for a moment because the system and rehab centers **"REJECT", ignore the delivering power of "the name of Jesus"** concerning addiction (see Acts 4:1-12). When Peter addressed the Sanhedrin (a high court of supreme counsels) after he had laid hands and healed many of diverse infirmities, they ask him**, "By what power, OR BY WHAT NAME, have ye done this"** (acts.4:7). Peter responded, **"Let it be known to all of you...that by the name of Jesus Christ the Nazarene, who you crucified, who God raised from the dead—BY THIS NAME this man stands before you in good health,"** delivered, healed, set free form the bondages and strongholds of life adversities, (see Acts 4:10 NASB).

The statement, **"The stone you builders rejected"** is also referring to today's founders, builders, and staff of drug treatment centers, who should be builders of the church but are rejecting the stone, Jesus Christ as the foundation of their establishment and their main goal of **"true deliverance"** (Jn.8:36) for its patients. The staff and founders of these rehabs instead suggest that their patients, clients refer to their source of deliverance by the name of "higher power" and other insignificant names. **When the Stone (Jesus) is perceived as worthless or having no real value people's lives are left to chance. The name of Jesus is a tried and tested weapon in our spiritual conflict.** Let us therefore stick to what works! The conclusion is that there is no other name by which diseased bodies can be cured, **so there is no other name by which sinful souls can be saved**!

Just as **"the man who had leprosy"** knelt down before Jesus and said, **"Lord you have the power to make me well"** (Lk.5: 12 CEV), and was delivered, we must all do in reference to our own spiritual leprosy's. We must first humble ourselves, as did the leper, and earnestly desire to be cleansed from adulteration, disease, and sin.

48

Most of all we must **firmly believe** Jesus' ability to cleanse, deliver us from the worlds defilement's, and when we apply ourselves to him we will find him very compassionate and ready to heal us. Notice that by one word, one touch from Christ *"the leprosy departed from the man"* (Lk.5:13). Dear reader, invite him into your life and he will do the same for you.

The Problem with Rehabilitation Centers and Their Programs

Now I'm not putting down the organizations and rehab centers that try to help people on drugs and alcohol, because they do offer some hope to their clients and patients by giving them a clean bed, good food to eat, and somewhat of a guideline to go by to combat the urges to use. But 99.9% of people who *"try to depend strictly"* on those ten, twelve, or fifteen step programs end up making several return trips if they don't end up in prison or dead. The problem that I have with man's so-called rehabilitation programs is that they are set up to please the world, *mainly due to financial greed.* Once I was stopped and told by a rehab administrator while giving an encouraging speech that I was not to tell their clients that they would not always be plagued by addiction. I simply said to them that, "Man says that you will always be an addicted, and that you'll never truly be free, but if the Son (Jesus) sets you free, then you are truly free indeed" (Jn.8:36).

The administrator walked me through the building while carefully pointing out the empty beds and said to me that they reason they instill in their patients, victims that they will always be fighting their addiction and truly never be free is because they need to believe this because if they—the rehab center—didn't have clients to fill their beds they would not get any funds or money to support their programs. His exact words were, *"we get two to three thousand dollars annually per man. But if we don't have a body in those beds we don't get the financial support."*

He then went on to tell me *not to say the name Jesus Christ,* but to refer to the name "higher power", thus insinuating that they don't want to offend anther's religious beliefs. But to be honest they (the rehab centers) are playing right into the hands of Satan by suggesting that those seeking deliverance use names such as, *"higher power",* when the Word of God plainly states, **"Only Jesus has the power to save! HIS NAME IS THE ONLY ONE IN ALL WORLD THAT CAN SAVE ANYONE!"** (Acts 4:12CEV; 19:11-17; 1Tim.2:5**)**. *Dear reader, there is only* **one name** *under heaven that has the power to save,* *and that name is not higher power or any other!* And as long as these institutions continue to *reject* THE ONLY NAME THAT THE DEVIL FEARS**, respects**, and *'trembles at"* (Js.2:19), the name SATAN RECOGNIZES THAT HAS THE POWER TO BREAK HIS STRONGHOLDS" (Acts 19:15) our households and neighborhoods will continue to portrait struggling crack cocaine addicts and other lost souls. (See Acts 3:6-8; 8:5-7; 16-16-18).

The devil realizes that if addicts ever come realize **"the power and authority"** (Lk.9:1; Mk.16:17) they have been commissioned with to overcome urges, temptations, and the pathetic lifestyle attached to drug addiction that his victims would become **"living testimonies"** (Rev.12: 17), and even **"begin to worshipped God"** *for their deliverance* (Acts3:6-9; Mk.5:6-15; Matt.8:2-3; 2Chr.20:1-3 ,17-22). The enemy is *afraid* that they will also become possible soul winners for the kingdom of God. This *fear* is the reason that the devil does all he can to keep his targets under the influence of drugs and alcohol. He of all people understands that "evil company corrupts good habits" (1Cor.15:33).

IT'S NO COINCIDENCE YOU'RE READING THIS BOOK, GOD KNOWS YOU'RE READY FOR A CHANGE

My friend, **it's no coincidence that this book is in your possession** at this present time. God knows that you are ready for a change! Psalms 139:1-17 clearly reveals that God knows all about your struggles. He knows that you are tired of living a pathetic life, tired of the sexual favors, tired of wandering the streets, sleeping outdoors, and struggling to make ends meet. Like the prodigal son "who wasted all his money on drugs, drinking, women, and wild living" you've got **to make a quality decision** to return to God, the Father (see Lk.11:17-22), and the Shepherd, Jesus, who's been waiting, looking for his lost sheep to answer the call of his voice (see Lk.15:4-10;Ezek.34:11-16;Jn.10:3,27).

The Devil Will Never Permanently Stop Trying To Tempt You

Your status does not carry any weight with temptation. The only assurance that you won't give in to sin or temptation is that you **remain a student of the Word**. Speaking of Satan's disrespect for a person's status our Lord and Savior, Jesus Christ, found out that after the devil *assumingly* stopped trying to tempt him, that it was only a matter of time before the enemy would return to try Him again. The Bible confirms that**, "After the devil had finished testing Jesus in every way possible, HE LEFT HIM FOR A WHILE**" (Lk.4: 13 CEV). Pay close attentions to those last three words: **"For a while".**

If you've ever been under sins control in any form or fashion, the devil knows about it, and he will wait, and wait, and wait**, "for the opportune time** "(Lk.4:13 NIV), when he thinks you're vulnerable to try and **"return unto the person from which the rebellious spirit was expelled"** (see Lk.11: 24).

My friend, it doesn't matter to the devil your position in life or your job title. Satan does not discriminate. He is very *patient.* And he is aware of every individual weakness. Just as Satan has the *patience* to wait on the right opportunity to catch you slipping, you need to develop *patience* for studying God's word to counter when he attacks!

"Put on the whole armor of God (STUDY THOSE VERSES IN REFERENCE TO YOUR DELIVERANCE), so that you will be able to stand up against the devil's temptations and lures" (Eph.6:11 TEV).

LIVE NO LONGER AS THE UNSAVED DO... (Eph.4: 17 LBV).

In the statement above, *"live no longer as the unsaved do"*, the apostle charged the Ephesians in the name and by the authority of the Lord Jesus, **that having professed the gospel, they should not be as the unconverted Gentiles, who walked in vain fancies and carnal affections.** Do not men, on every side, walk in the vanity of their minds? Must not we then urge the distinction between real and nominal Christians? **They were void of all saving knowledge; they sat in darkness, and loved it** rather than light. <u>**They had a dislike and hatred to a life of holiness,**</u> which is not only the way of life God requires and approves, and by which we live to him, but which has some likeness to God himself in his purity, righteousness, truth, and goodness. Sinful desires are deceitful lusts; they promise men happiness, but render them more miserable; and bring them to destruction, if not subdued and mortified and **therefore must be put off, as an old garment, a filthy garment; they must be subdued and mortified.**

But it is not enough to shake off corrupt principles; we must have gracious ones. **By the new man, is meant the new nature, the new creature, directed by a new principle, even regenerating grace, enabling a man to lead a new life of righteousness and holiness. This is created, or brought forth by God's almighty power.**

Don't Go To Wild Parties

(Rom.13:12 CEV)

"So I tell you this, and *insist on it* in the Lord, **that you must no longer live Like those who don't care about pleasing God do...** They are darkened in their understanding and separated from the life of God **BECAUSE OF THE IGNORANCE THAT IS IN THEM DUE TO THE HARDENING OF THEIR HEARTS"** (Eph.4:17-18 NIV).

4

PRAYER WHEN TEMPTED TO BUY CRACK TODAY

*D*EAR reader, the first thing I want you to realize is that **it's not a sin to be tempted, it's only a sin if you actually commit or give in to the transgression.**

Blessed (happy, to be envied) is the man who is patient under trial and stands up under temptation, for when he has stood the test and been approved, he will receive [the victor's] crown of life which God has promised to those who love Him (Js.1:12 AMP).

The Bible tells us that **"temptation is common to man"** (1Cor.10:13), meaning that we should expect to be tempted in certain areas of our lives, but we don't have to give in to the appeal. The Bible reveals Satan as **"the tempter"** (Matt.4:3; 1Thess.3:5), a, *morally wrong, corrupt* spirit that *"beguiles and deceives mankind into committing sin"* (see Rev.12:9; 13:14; 19:20), however he (the devil) **does not have any real power to Make us give in to the disobedience.**

How does Satan accomplish the task of getting people to sin, use drugs, or commit other things that God detest?

The answer is that since Satan does not possess **omniscience** (unlimited knowledge), nor **omnipresence** (the ability to be everywhere at the same time) as the "All

Knowing, Almighty God does (see Deu.31:21; Rev.19:6), Satan simply has to depend on the intelligence he gets from the *"one-third"* surplus of other fallen angels who were cast out of heaven with him (Rev.12:4, 9) concerning specific weaknesses in the lives of certain individuals, and with that information he plans a similar attack to the one he utilize on Eve in the garden of Eden, and the end result is that our responses is normally the same one Eve gave: **"... The serpent beguiled (cheated, outwitted) and deceived me"** (Gen.3:13 AMP). Yes, Satan may be to blame, *but the final decision* is up to you to eat the forbidden fruit (Gen.2:15-17; 3:1-6), smoke dope, fornicate, commit adultery, kill, or steal, the list goes on. Eve's reply is proof that Satan does not have any real power to *make us* sin and therefore he stoops to **"Lies"** (Gen.3:4), **trickery** (Gen.3:6), **DECEPTION** (Gen.3:1, 13), **"Envy** and **lust"** (Gen.3:5, 6) to play with our limitations, thoughts, and desires.

Christ Was Faced With The Same Temptations But He Had A Secret To Not Giving In To Them.

What was Christ's secret to not holding out and not giving in to temptations! Well, to be honest he didn't have a secret. He simply understood the power and authority that God's Written Word carries when spoken in the face of temptations, the enemy, sin's offering! Just as Satan took advantage of Eve's *ignorance* concerning God's commands (Gen.2:15), her *weakness* for certain foods, and *eye* for beauty (Gen.3:6) he's still up to his old **tricks** today by using a person's **"ignorance"**(Lev.4:2, 13, 22, 27; 1Tim.1: 13) against them and most of all "the power of God's word" when spoken to overcome certain temptations, weaknesses and cravings for food, alcohol, drugs, sexuality immorality and other sins. Christ overcame

Satan's temptations by using the Written Word of God! It's why every time Satan tried to get him to give in to temptation Jesus said, *"IT IS WRITTEN..."*, before he quoted the actual bible verse that was empowered to give him strength to say no to sin! (See Lk.4:4, 8,12).

That same written word of God is available to us today! But if we don't know what God's written word has to say about particular temptations and "the power it holds" which gives us the ability and strength to say no to sin then we will always remain a victim to temptation. When a person speaks God's Word it's actually God's Holy Spirit speaking through that person which gives the spoken word life and power! And since God himself lives in his word thereby giving the spoken word "power and life" then he who speaks the word speaks life! The Written Word is truly part of God Himself, because God lives in his Word! And so when we as Christians speak the Written Word, mixed with faith, it carries the same power and authority as it did when Jesus spoke it in Luke 4:1-13 when he was tempted. That's why Jesus said, *"But fear not. You too can overcome the devil's temptations, enticements.* **"In this world you will have trouble (will be faced with temptations). But take heart! I have overcome the world"** (Jn.16:33 NIV).

"He was tempted in every way just as we are yet he did not give in" (Heb.4:15; Lk.4:2 NIV). Christ didn't give in because his **love for the word** *of God (Lk.2:46-49;5:17)*, to **perform the will** *of God* (Jn.4:34;6:38-39) and **please God** *in his everyday life* (Matt.3:17; Rom.15:3; 2Tim.2:4;1Thess.4:1;Gal.1:10) **WAS STRONGER THAN THE DESIRE TO SIN... TO FORNICATE, COMMIT ADULTERY...TO USE.**

Just as Jesus realized that God promises that every written word of spoken in trust and in faith *"will not return void but accomplish what he sent it out to do"* (Isa. 55: 10-11), that God would *"watch over his word to perform it"* (Jer.1:12), and that God *"promises to fulfill his word when we speak it"* (**Num.23:19**) then we start to realized it too we will also have victory over temptations of our flesh! The plain truth is that, *"the Word is alive"* (Heb.4:12) and if we won't to put a stop to living like the walking dead then we've got to learn how to speak life over our dead situations. If it wasn't for unbelief, lack of faith in God's word you would be free a long time ago.

Now you might be saying to yourself, " I pray, I believe, but it doesn't work for me." Do you know why? It's because according to Mk. 4:15 the devil has stolen your faith in the Word of God and the prayer you pray for deliverance, prosperity, a job, and so on! Some of you might say, *"well, I'm not Jesus, and so don't expect me to be as strong"*. My reply to you is, "Jesus wrestled with weakness at times too" (see Heb.4:15) especially when it came to *choice* of giving up the calling, staying here on earth and enjoying life's pleasures (Matt.26:39, 41), or "doing the will of God" (Matt.26:42) by dying, in our place, "that we might be saved!"

"Therefore being justified by faith, we have peace with God through our Lord Jesus Christ...For when we were yet without strength, in due time Christ died for the ungodly... (Rom.5:1, 6). Jesus had a choice to make and he chose to honor the Word and will of God.

Have you ever heard someone say, **"The devil made me do it"** after committing an offense? Well, **the** truth is that the devil can't **MAKE** you do anything; he can only suggest it to you. The final result is that it's up to you to go along with the *suggestion* or you can decide to REBUKE (Mk.1:23-25; 8:32; Tit. 1:10-13), and BIND that evil spirit of blasphemy (Matt.12:29; 16:19). However, there will always be some like the "*one-third*" of those angels and "*Eve*" (see Gen. 3:13; Rev.12:4) who each gave in to the suggestions of Satan, ignoring the fact that they were willfully giving into sin which leads to what is known as making a nonsensical *choice.*

My friend, all the temptations in life that you will ever be faced with come down to the *choices that you decide to make* and it's why Joshua stated: **"Now therefore fear the LORD, and serve him in sincerity... And if it seems evil unto you to serve the LORD, <u>choose you this day </u>whom ye will serve... but as for me and my house, we will serve the LORD"** (Josh.24:14-15). Again it all comes down to the *gift that God has given us called* choice.

The Choice To Accept Satan's Principles Or God's Is Yours

The Scofield Study Bible annotations in reference to Rev.13:8 with regard to our *choosing* who we "*wilt fall down and worship*", God or Satan (see Matt.4:8-10) informs us by stating: "*In the sense of* **the present world system** the **ethically bad** (those who do not honor the word of God in their lives) **refer to the order** of arrangement **under which Satan *has organized*** *the world of* **unbelieving mankind under his** cosmic **principles** of *force, greed, selfishness, ambition, and* sinful pleasure (Matt.4:8-9; Eph:2: 2;6:12; 1Jn. 2:15-17).

The world system is imposing...DOMINATED BY SATANIC PRINCIPLES (the same *principles* he wanted to govern heaven under prior to losing the battle and being cast out). The world system is often **outwardly religious**...but enraged with national and commercial rivalries...**dominated by satanic principles**".

What A Big Difference Between God's Principles And Satan's

On the other hand GOD'S PRINCIPLES, as well as his *will* is for the inhabitants of heaven is for us to live a life of tranquility, peace, joy, happiness, and above all LOVE towards one another:

"This is my commandment, That ye love one another, as I have loved you... These things I command you, that ye love one another (Jn.15:12, 17).

"Master, which is the great commandment in the law? Jesus said unto him, Thou shalt love the Lord thy God with all thy heart, and with all thy soul, and with all thy mind. This is the first and great commandment. And the second is like unto it, Thou shalt love thy neighbour as thyself. On these two commandments hang all the law... (Matt.22:36-40).

"Owe no man anything, but to love one another: for he that loveth another hath fulfilled the law... Love worketh no ill to his neighbour: therefore love is the fulfilling of the law" (Rom.13:8,10).

"Thou shalt not hate thy brother in thine heart" (Lev19:17).

60

What a big difference between the principles of Satan's And God's? Nevertheless God leaves the **choice** up to you! The Bible gives another illustration of the gift of choice when the children of Israel **decided** that they no longer wanted God's appointed judges to *govern* over them (1Sam.7:15-17; 8:1, 19), *teaching* them the will of God, but preferred a king so that they could live like the other nation who did not reverence God in their lives (1Sam.8:6), and the end result of their *choice* was not what they expected (see 1Sam.8:7-22).

The finale of the matter is **that you cannot expect God results living a godless life!** My friend, in order for you to be able to make the correct choices in life you're going to need *the shield of faith, the helmet of salvation, and the sword of the Spirit, which is the word of God.*

"Finally, let the mighty strength of the Lord make you strong. Put on all the armor that God gives, so you can defend yourself against the devils tricks...So put on all the armor that God gives. Then when that evil day comes, you will be able to defend yourself. And when the battle is over, you will still be standing firm. Let your faith be like a shield, and you will be able to stop all the flaming arrows of the evil one. Let God's saving power be like a helmet, and for a sword use God's message **(God's Word) that comes from the Spirit"** (Eph.6:10-11, 13, 16-17 CEV).

Study the word of God to find out what sort of life pleases Him, and then pray for God's Holy Spirit to help you make those changes!

Christ understands perfectly well that we too that will be face with temptations (Lk.4:1-13; Jn.16:33; Heb.4:15) and that's why he tells us to do what he had to do to overcome and that is to **"Watch, pray…"** (Matt.26:41), and counter temptation with *"It is written"* (see Matt. 4:4, 7, 10; Ex20:1-24), thereby **allowing "the anointing of God's word to destroy the yoke of bondage"** (Isa.10:27*)*.

"In this manner… Therefore, pray…lead us not into temptation but deliver us from evil" (Matt.6:9, 13).

My friend, everyday upon awakening, especially before you go out the door to work or play immediately fall to your knees and pray:

"Don't let me do wrong on purpose Lord, don't let sin have control over me. Keep me from presumptuous sins. Gird me with your anointing and strength so that I won't give in or be overpowered by my own fleshly, sinful desires. Overshadow me with the same Godly Spirit and anointing that gave Christ the strength to say no to temptation while he was on earth. Keep me, O Lord, from the hands of the wicked: preserve me from the violent man; who have purpose to overthrow my goings. Here me speedily, O Lord: my spirit faileth: hide not thy face from me, lest I be like unto them that go down into the pit". (See Ps.19: 13; 18:32; Isa.40:29; Ps.84: 5; 105: 5; 86:16; Eph.2:1-5; Lk.4:1-13; Ps.104:4; 143:7). In Jesus name I pray. Amen.

As you go throughout your day I want you to keep in mind that when temptation arises **it's only Satan playing with your thoughts** and sinful desires with the hope that *"you will give in to those lustful irreligious yearnings"*. The book of James confirms that **"We are**

62

tempted by our own desires that drag us off and trap us. Our desires make us sin, and when sin is finished with us, it leaves us dead. (Js.1:14-15).

My friend, when those wicked thoughts enter your mind IMMEDIATELY say to them, **"Greater, more Powerful is the Spirit of Christ living in me, and strengthening me** (1Jn.4:4), **than that of Satan's, which is "The spirit at work in the hearts of those who refuse to obey God** "(Eph.2:2NLT) trying manipulate and deceive me into using, backsliding, sinning against God" (1Jn.4:4). Thank you Lord that your word declares, **"Fear not, for I am with you...I will strengthen you, Yes, I will help you".** (See Isa.41:10; Job 4:3-4; Ps.31:4; 119:28). Amen.

I'M GETTING WEAK LORD NOW WHAT AM I SUPPOSED TO DO

If you really want to be free from the suggestions, urges and cravings for crack cocaine you're going to have to daily **"CAST DOWN THOSE EVIL IMAGINATIONS (thoughts, propositions) that attempt to exalt themselves against God's will for you to be blessed, saved, *delivered,* set free!** (See 1Cor.10:13; 1Tim.2:4; Jn.3:17). In the words of the Apostle Paul, **"I die daily"** (1Cor.15:31) to sin.

Paul goes on to say, **"We are hedged in (pressed) on every side [troubled and oppressed in every way], but not cramped or crushed; we suffer embarrassments and are perplexed and unable to find a way out, but not driven to despair; We are pursued (persecuted and hard driven), but not deserted [to stand alone]; we are struck down to the ground, but never struck out and destroyed;**

Christianity is a process, choosing to be free or not to give to that which we know is sin is a PROCESS. **"Though our inner man is PROGRESSIVELY decaying and wasting away, yet our inner self is being PROGRESSIVELY renewed day by day"** (2Cor.4:16), And for that reason the word of God is there to help you achieve that process, **"to make you wise enough to have faith in Christ Jesus and be saved....It is useful for teaching and helping people and for correcting them and showing them how to live"** (2Tim 3:15-16 CEV).

Jesus understands what it's like *"to be tempted with evil"* (Heb.4:15), and for that reason he has promised that **"he will not let you be tempted and tried and assayed beyond your ability and strength of resistance and power to endure, *but with the temptation* He will [always] also provide the way out (the means of escape to a landing place), that you may be capable and strong and powerful to bear up under it patiently"** (1Cor.10:13 AMP).

The SPIRIT OF CHRIST ABIDING IN YOU IS THE STRONGER ENTITY

On that note you simply need to **remind God of those promises To deliver you** because He's not going to force himself on anyone who doesn't HUMBLY ask for his support. God has given us *the gift of choice* and because the Word tells us that we're waged in a spiritual war against the **temptations of Satan** our best strategy, like that of the military, is to build up a defense system against the enemy. *"How do I accomplish that"* you ask?

64

By first honestly recognizing your own individual weaknesses in reference to sin, your desires, lusts (2Cor.13:5), and **then locating the promises in God's written word that attribute to victory!** If you would begin and end each day on your knees the closer your personal relationship will be with Christ, and as a result your resistance to sin will become stronger. According to Luke 4:13 Satan won't give up his mission of luring you into sin, so it's up to you not to give up your preparation for his attacks by sincerely making God's word your life line (see Eph.6:11-17).

My friend, when you stand before the judgment seat of God and Christ you will have to answer for **"every secret thing done, whether it be good, or whether it be evil"** (Eccl.12:13-14). So don't get stuck standing before God with an *"if-I-da"* face. In other words don't get caught *"standing before the judgment seat of God"* (see Rev.20:11-15) and right before ruling God asks you "why didn't repent of a certain sin" and you're standing there thinking, "If I would of said no; if I would of got out of that sinful relationship; if I would of just did what the Word". My friend, don't get caught with the *"if-Ida"* face.

*Blessed (happy, fortunate, and to be envied) are those servants whom the master finds awake and alert and watching when he comes. Truly I say to you, he will gird himself and have them recline at table and will come and serve them... But if that servant says in his heart, My master is late in coming, and begins to strike the menservants and the maids and to eat and drink and get drunk,

The master of that servant will come on a day when he does not expect him and at an hour of which he does not know, and will punish him and cut him off and assign his lot with the unfaithful. And that servant who knew his master's will but did not get ready or act as he would wish him to act shall be beaten with many [lashes].

But he who did not know and did things worthy of a beating shall be beaten with few [lashes]". (Lk.12:37, 45-48 AMP)

65

It's time For You To Start Fighting Back With The Word

It's time to suit up warrior! It's time to **"put on the whole armor of God that ye may be able to stand against the wiles (tricks) of the devil".** It's time for you, dear reader, to learn how to reject Satan's suggestions to use or give into sin by retaliating with the **"sword of the Spirit, which is the word of God "**(Eph.6: 11, 17).

There's only one guaranteed way that you will ever be able to defeat and overcome the suggestion of Satan, and that is by **IMMEDIATELY** referring to the written Word of God when demonic seeds of enticement enter the mind.

The fine print of God's *guarantee* reads, "**For the Word that God speaks is alive and full of power** [making it active, operative, energizing, and effective]...penetrating to the dividing line of the breath of life (soul) and [the immortal] spirit, and of joints and marrow [of the deepest parts of our nature], exposing and sifting and analyzing and judging the very thoughts and purposes of the heart"** (Heb.4:12 AMP). What a guarantee!

The following scenarios offer powerful verses from the Word of God to combat the temptations to use or engage in other rebellious acts that the enemy knows does not please God. Apply them to your life and reap the benefits of blessings and deliverance!

SCENARIO:

Today is payday. You've gone all week long without using drugs, but today there has been an ongoing

66

war waging in your mind—the urge to use and not wanting to: **"The sinful nature does not want what the Spirit delights in. And the Spirit does not want what the sinful nature delights in. THE TWO ARE AT WAR WITH EACH OTHER.** That's what make you do what you don't want to do"** (Gal.5: 17 NIV).

All day long the demon of crack cocaine "suggestion" (Gen.3: 1-5) has been trying to override your will to resist. It seems the more you contest the thoughts of using, the stronger the urges become.

Suddenly the devil begins to whisper things like: *"Don't worry about it. This time you're in control of the situation. You won't be as stupid as you were the last time, and spend up all your money. You understand now that you have responsibilities so you have to limit yourself.*
You can do it. You're not as weak as it may appear. Just buy one crack-rock and maybe a cold beer and that will be it. But first you need to separate your bill money from your spare money. And don't touch it no matter what! Come on, you can do this!"

Sound familiar? Well, by now you should know that crack cocaine does not cooperate with well-meaning plans. It has no conscience or sympathy. On that note allow me to share this parable:

There was a man who was in the bathtub. The tub was filled with crack cocaine. The man gradually smoked each one until the bathtub was nearly empty. When he finally finished smoking the last one, he said to himself, "If I just had one more I'll be satisfied."

Please, meditate on what you just read. The truth is that when it comes to crack cocaine, **ONE IS TOO MANY AND A THOUSAND IS NEVER ENOUGH!**

The point is that the cravings for crack cocaine are nearly impossible to satisfy once you use. Therefore, when these intriguing thoughts of using attempted to invade your peace of mind, rebuke the devil's offer by *IMMEDIATEL*Y responding,

POWER PRAYER

It is written, **"There hath no temptation taken you such as is common to man: but God is faithful who will not suffer you to be tempted above that ye are able; but will with the temptation also make a way to escape, that ye may be able to bear it"** (1Cor.10: 13).

Now in your own words say something like, *"The sinful desires and thoughts I'm experiencing are common. But God is faithful, and I can depend on Him to stand by his promise not to let me be overpowered by the enticement to use. Thank you, God for the promise to also make a way for me to escape. I admit that I know entertaining the thought of using is wrong because my spirit is fighting against my flesh (Gal.5:17). I truly want to do Your will as far as my rededicated heart is concern, but my old sinful nature is telling me to do the very thing I'm seeking deliverance from. Who will free me from my servitude to sin, the addiction and dependence on crack and alcohol? Thank God it's already been done by Jesus Christ my Lord! It is by His Spirit that I am strengthened and set free from the pathetic, ignorant, enticement of crack cocaine! (See Rom.7:17-25 LBV).* **By the power of the blood of Jesus** *my thoughts(the thoughts of using) are being purged from dead works, my conscience is being cleared so that I may serve the living God and no longer do the things I use to do (see Heb.9:14 CEV).* **"In the name of Jesus"** *(see Rom.10:9; Acts 4:10-12) I pray. Amen. .*

Praising God Contributes To Lasting Victory

REMEMBER to always **PRAISE** God like Jehoshaphat and the people of Judah did when they were about to be *attacked* by several adversaries (2 Chr.20:1-2). It was only after *"seeking God in prayer"* (2Chr.20:5), that God told him that he *didn't have to fight* (v.17), <u>that all Jehoshaphat had to do was PRAISE Him,</u> **"And when they began to sing and Praise, the Lord sent and ambush..."** (v.22).

68

In the spirit of Jehoshaphat it would benefit you to also praise God as the urges to use grow stronger. The more intense the urge grows, the louder you BEGIN TO SING AND PRAISE God. In the words of the Psalmist, *"I will call upon the Lord, WHO IS WORTHY TO BE PRAISED: so shall I be saved from my enemies"* *(Ps.18: 3).*

Whenever the Psalmist felt he was about to be overpowered by adversity or temptation he learned that the secret to walking away in victory was to **"PRAISE GOD MORE AND MORE"** (Ps.71: 14).

Lord Give Me Twice The Strength To Defeat This Habit

I want you to also realize that there are certain demon spirits *"that can only be expelled except by fasting and prayer"* (See Matt.17:21). These are those nasty *habits* or *spirits* that you've been *wrestling* with the longest. Just as Elisha asked God for a *double portion* of anointing (see 2Kgs.2:9), we too can be strengthen *with twice the power* to overcome temptations by giving ourselves to fasting and prayer.

Fasting and prayer are proper means for the bringing down of Satan's power or strongholds over us, and for tapping in on God's divine intervention and power to assist us in our BATTLES AND quests.

Fasting is used to put and edge on prayer; *it is an evidence of humiliation which is necessary in prayer,* and is a means of mortifying some corrupt habit and disposing the body to serve the soul in prayer. WHEN THE DEVIL'S INTREST IN ONE'S CHARACTER IS CONFIRMED BY THAT PERSON BEING TEMPTED, FASTING MUST BE JOINED WITH PRAYER TO KEEP THE FLESH UNDER SUBMISSION.

5

PRAYERS WHEN LIVING IN DRUG RIDDEN NEIGHBORHOODS

If you are going through what I went through during my *"SPELL"* (Acts16:16, 18) of crack cocaine addiction by unfortunately having to living in or nearby a drug infested neighborhood, I know that it is not easy trying to quit while surrounded by such temptation and evil companions. . The Bible gives an account of these demonic territorial spirits seeking certain neighborhoods and districts to set up shop in. Notice in Mark 5:8-10 that after Christ rebuked the evil spirits out of the man, they, *"the demon spirits BEGGED Jesus not to send them out of that neighborhood..." (v.12).* This verse alone proves that demon spirits do have a preference about the neighborhoods they want to canvas and that they don't care what sort of body *"they possess"* (human or animal) just as long as they are able to cause some type of mayhem through the instrument.

But praise God that His Word promises that **"he will cause the evil beast (the drug dealers and users) to cease from the land** (your neighborhood), **and you shall dwell in safety. That he will save you, and you will no longer be spoiled by the beast of prey** (you won't pawn your car, television or jewelry for drugs, your hard earn money won't be given to the drug dealers); **that you enjoy a Holy security under the divine protection of**

70

the Shepherd, who has rid the land of wild beast, having vanquished all our spiritual enemies! Sin and Satan, death and hell. **Through Christ, God Deliverers His Children Not Only From The People And Things That They Have Reason To Fear, but from the fear of even death itself! (See Ezek. 34: 11-16, 22-31).** Praise God, dear reader, that by "**the same way that He watched over, protected and saved Ezra from enemies and bandits that lurked as he traveled through certain regions, neighborhoods**" (see Ezra 8:31) he will also protect, save and watch over you as you journey through the neighborhood.

Do you want that kind of protection? Then all you have to do is **simply "remind, put God in remembrance of his promises to escort, watch over and protect you from the enemies and bandits that lurk** (the drug dealers lurking on the street corner and in the allies, the thieves hiding and waiting for a chance to rob you...) **so that you may be justified, supported by the facts**"(see Isa. 43:26). Even the common perils of our journey's and travels oblique us to sanctify our going out with prayer and our returns in peace with praise and thanksgiving. Just as **"ISRAEL SANG, DANCED AND PRAISED GOD FOR THEIR DELIVERANCE FROM THE BONDAGE OF SLAVERY AND THE PURSUIT OF PHARAOH AND HIS ARMY"** (see Ex.14:30-31; 15:1-12) , it is well also in our favor sanctify our going and returning safely with songs of praise and thanksgiving.

This Neighborhood Is Contributing To My Weakness

When it comes to considering the neighborhood that you will be moving into if you're like most people you try to find the least expensive place to live with a few benefits like lack of drug traffic. But in some cases there are those who have to simply settle for what their finances will allow, and nine times out of ten drug traffic is evident. The users in the neighborhood are normally stressed out with life and at times they just need something to set their minds aside from problems which occur in their everyday life. There are many reasons as to why people are sometimes force into moving into a community or neighborhood that's fighting to cleanse the area as well as the reason why most people use drugs. In the business of ministry I found that the main reason people use drugs is because they don't socialize with the normal, god-fearing people around them.

They believe that the further away they are from the rest of the world the better they are. As time goes by, these people who have no real guidance like people in their circle who don't use drugs they begin to believe that they can ease run away from their problems by smoking or sniffing drugs. Furthermore they believe that the more drugs they buy from others, the more friends they make. They don't realize that the more drugs they share and buy the more they are socializing in the wrong way. As a testimony, I remember that every time I made up my mind not to use that day, the devil would tactically send someone to my house or around me who would allude to using. To be honest I can't remember how many times I sincerely made up my mind not to use that day but failed. It was only until I was made aware of the fact that **all drug infested neighborhoods are under the control**

and influence of Satan (see Rev.18:2;1Chr.21:1;Ex.32:1,6;Matt.13:37-39;Prov.7:5-12,22-27) that I began to shield myself in prayer against any assault Eph.6:11-17. **I learned to put on my armor every day before I got out of bed, and before retiring by thanking God for his grace and protection** (see Eph.6:10-18).

Moses understood the realism of neighborhoods being seized by evil spirits and before he moved into a certain district he sent spies to survey the area to make sure that where they would be living would be an ideal place. (See Num 13:1-2, 16-33.)

All DRUG INFESTED NEIGHBORHOODS ARE UNDER THE CONTROL OF SATAN.

The truth of certain neighborhoods being under demonic control can be found concerning Sodom and Gomorrah, where that particular neighborhood was under the watchful eye of demon *"spirits of perversion and rebellion"* (see Gen.13: 10; 19:1-14). In 1st Pet.5:8). Furthermore we are again told that *"the devil is walking around, surveying neighborhoods, and looking for victims"* (1Pet.5:8). Also in Job 1:6-7 we are informed of *"Satan's attentive eye"* in search of people and neighborhoods to vandalize.

The book of Isaiah as well relates to those *"perverse spirits"* canvassing certain neighborhoods causing people living in those areas *to walk in error* (Isa.19: 14). Let's not forget about the *"prince of Tyrus"* and the region that he governed. According the Matthew Commentary On The Whole Bible", we are told that every *conceited* decision that the *"Prince of Tyrus"* made in reference to the welfare of that community *was support by demonic influence:* **"He was possessed and guided by Satan, like many of the**

73

arrogant **rulers of third world countries are today**. (See Ezk.28: 12).

The Scofield Study Bible referring to Isaiah 14:12-14 supports by adding, **"Verses 12-14 evidently refer to Satan,** who as prince of this world system, is **THE REAL THOUGH UNSEEN RULER** of the successive world powers", "spiritual bodies invisible to the natural eye"** (2Kg.6:16-17;Col.1:16;Heb.11:27)

The point is that wherever there's any kind of drug activity or signs of sexuality immorality *"demonic spirits of rebellion"* (Ezr.4:12; 15), assign to those neighborhoods by Satan are the guilty parties behind the irreligious behavior of those victimized because, **"It is his (Satan's) spirit that has power over everyone who doesn't obey God"** (Eph.2:2 CEV).

Remember that we're not called to fight our adversaries; we are simply to become aware, face, and then overcome his stratagems by the referring to the power of the written word of God. That's why we are told to **"put on the whole armor of God in order to stand against the tricks of the devil...to take the helmet of salvation and the sword of the Spirit, which is the word of God"** (Eph.6:11,17).

"This is what the LORD says to you: 'Do not be afraid or discouraged... For the battle is not yours, but God's... You will not have to fight this battle. Take up your positions; stand firm and see the deliverance the LORD will give...Do not be afraid; do not be discouraged. Go out to face them tomorrow, and the LORD will be with you.' "(2Chr.20:15-17 NIV).

SCENARIO:

You are walking through the local neighborhood, and all things to be considered feeling good about past accomplishments. However, the awareness of drug activity is evident: the dealers hanging out on the corners and in the back allies, crack user's walking around like zombies while looking for drugs, the prostitutes, whores and homeless characterizing the area.

It seems like everywhere you turn and the more you try to disregard the activities the more subliminal messages Satan has posted along the way…

POWER PRAYER

Regardless, whenever your surroundings intensify the urge to use IMMEDIATELY respond, **"Though I walk in the midst of trouble, thou wilt revive me: thou shalt stretch forth thine hand against the wrath of mine enemies, and thy right hand shall save me"** (Ps.138:7)

"Yea, thou I walk through the valley of the shadow of death (the crack neighborhood), I will fear no evil for thou (Jesus) art with me" (Ps.23.4).

After quoting the verse in its original dialect **say in your own words something like:** *"Although I live in this neighborhood. A neighbor that portraits the shadow of death (crack activity) I am no longer afraid of what surrounds me. I fear no evil… because today I welcome Jesus to walk along beside me. As a dear friend, and stronger companion He will not allow any weakness to overpower me. Therefore, I will not be so easily enticed or disturbed by the activity around me. The Spirit of Christ strengthens me. No longer do I walk the path of sinners (other struggling crack users).*

I must refrain my feet from following their path (looking for crack dealers or a secluded place to smoke) because their intentions are only evil. For stronger is the Spirit of Christ living in me (1Jn.4:4), *than the demonic influential spirit of Satan that's trying to deceive me. Hallelujah! Hallelujah! Hallelujah!*

Thank You, Lord, for strengthening me with power to overcome such times of temptation. In the name of Jesus Christ, the source of my strength, and my deliverer, I pray. Amen.

Now Lift Your Hands In Praise

After you finishing praying lift your hands in the surrender position, began to sing and praise God for strengthening you! If you have access to a phone call a friend or support partner and share your testimony. The best outcome would be to go the person's house you're sharing testimony with or have them to come over which will add strength to your declaration.

Just as Satan needs the support of the *"one-third"* fallen angels that *"misleadingly joined Satan in the battle to overthrow God's throne"* (Rev.12:4,7-10;Isa.14:12-15) who are now known as *"evil spirits",* (Lk.8:2) *"seducing spirits"* (1Tim.4:1), *"spirits of devils"* (Rev.16:14) *"...evil spirits in the heavenly places"* (Eph.6:12 NLT) that roam the earth to undermine the salvation of man, we need each other's spiritual SUPPORT to strengthen us in times of weakness. That's the reason *"...Jesus called together his twelve apostles and sent them out two by two..."* (Mk.6:7 CEV). If one ever became weak, the other was there for moral support!

"Two are better than one; because they have a good reward..." (Eccl.4:9).

6

PRAYERS TO REBUKE THE IDEA OF STEALING

Another phase I've found to be evident in the lives of people recovering from drug addiction and attempting rededication to Christ, is that although the person may have overcome sins like cursing, fornication, lust, to name a few, that same person, who wants to be a good Christian may still battle with the compulsion to steal.

Why? Because they have not been delivered from *the spirit of thievery* (Jn.10: 10).When it comes to Christianity many people are led to think that once you get saved all your struggles are over. Well, the truth is that just because a person has decided to dedicate their life to Christ it doesn't mean they are immune to sin. That person simply has to **"work harder on becoming a better representative as a follower of Christ"** according to 2Cor.5:20, and Colossians 3:1-10. *In the process of working harder, praying for deliverance is a necessity.*

You're Still Struggling Because You're
Saved **But** Not Delivered

What am I talking about when I say a person can be saved but not delivered? For example, a person may be saved but still struggle with smoking cigarettes. However, it doesn't mean that person is not saved, as some hypocrites might think, it simply means that person has not *delivered* from the spirit of nicotine. You might say, "How can a person claim to save but still have a tendency to curse at times?" The answer again is because they, their **"tongue has not been delivered"** from the spirit of blasphemy (Ps.120:2; 34:13; 66:17; Rev.13:6).

Pray For Deliverance In Correlation To Your Salvation

There are many scholars, preachers, and teachers of the bible who will argue that salvation and deliverance are one in the same, and there is a very thin line. Nevertheless, when it comes to our own PERSONAL struggles, especially with crack cocaine, critics need to understand what the writer was insinuating when he said, "WORK OUT YOUR OWN SALVATION WITH FEAR AND TREMBLING" (Phil.2: 12).

IT'S TIME FOR YOU TO BREAK THOSE
SELF-DEFEATING HABITS.

There are certain character defects and self-defeating habits that we all need to *"work out"* in *fear* of the Lord, when it comes to being delivered from. King David understood this need to *"work out"*, or "work on" certain areas in his life that called for delivered. That's why you'll find in many of the Psalms David not only praying to be saved, but praying for deliverance. (See Ps.37:40; 71:2; 72:13; 106:47).

"Keep back (deliver) thy servant from presumptuous sins..." (Ps.19: 13).

"Deliver me from workers of iniquity..." (Ps. 59:2).

"Have mercy upon me O Lord; for I am weak... Return, O Lord, deliver my soul... (Ps.6: 2, 4).

My friend, when it comes to understanding the battle of recovering from a sexual immoral, drug *(crack)* addicted lifestyle there are many dark areas of behavior that need to be exposed and relinquished if one expect to be 'truly free" (Jn.8:36).

In this case the compulsion to steal is what we're dealing with. Satan, whom the bible classifies as a thief (Jn.10: 10) ignites this pattern of behavior (Jn.10: 10).

THE REASON MANY PEOPLE CONTINUE TO STRUGGLE IN CERTAIN AREAS IS BECAUSE THEY'RE AT WAR WITH THEIR OLD REBELLIOUS NATURE

The reason that many people seeking recovery and rededication to Christ continue to struggle in this area is because *"the old demonic, rebellious, disobedient, spirit that once had control of their soul is at war with their desire to change for the better* (see Eph.2:2; Galatians 5:17; 1Peter2: 11).

People combating drug addiction or homelessness appear to struggle more with the obsession to steal because the years of living by the so-called "code of survival" — stealing and doing whatever it takes to support their habit — has allowed Satan to *darken* (Jn.12: 35) precise areas of spiritual reasoning (Eph.4: 18) when it comes to the severity of the offence toward God (see Acts 24: 16).

I Know It's Wrong Lord But...

For instance, many victims are incline to overlook the consequences of things like taking a newspaper off someone's front lawn, picking up a pencil of someone's desk, a book from the library. Removing toiletry from

79

public restrooms; salt and pepper shakers from restaurants, or deceiving people out of money that will eventually be used to buy drugs. The list goes on.

When a person steals it's like saying to God, "I know it's wrong, but I don't have the patience or time to wait around to see if you are going to bless me with this particular item. So I'll do it Satan's way and steal it".

Dear Reader, stealing is an insult towards God's trust to *"supply all your needs"* (Phil.4: 19). Satan understands also that stealing reveals a lack of faith and that ***"it is impossible to please God without faith. Anyone who comes to him must believe that there is a God and that he REWARDS those who sincerely seek him"*** (Heb.11: 6 NLB).

Stop Letting Satan Influence You To Steal.

Please, stop allowing Satan to suggest, influence you to steal. It is not the will of God. He will provide as he always has from the beginning of creation. He hasn't change (Mal.3: 6). He is the same yesterday, today, and forever (Heb.13: 8).

When God said to Elijah, *"Go east and hide in the Kerith Valley…I HAVE ORDERED SOME RAVENS TO FEED YOU THERE"* (1Kg.17: 3-4 NIV), then afterwards arranged for a "stranger", a widow woman to come into his life in order to assist him on the journey (1Kg.17: 8-16); and provided for the children of Israel while they were wandering in the desert (Ex, 16:4, 15; Deu.8: 4). Then that same God will provide for you because **HE'S THE SAME GOD YESTERDAY, TODAY, AND FOREVER.** (Heb.13:8). If for whatever reason you find yourself entertaining thoughts of committing robbery or stealing, even if it's something as simple as taking two newspapers out of the stand for the price of one, IMMEDIATELY respond:

POWER PRAYER

It is written, **"Thou shalt not steal"** (Ex.20: 15).

"If a man shall steal an ox, or a sheep, and kill it, or sell it; he shall restore five oxen for an ox, and four sheep for a sheep" (Ex.21:1).

"Ye shall not steal, neither deal falsely, neither lie one to another" (Lev.19:11).

"You shall not rob nor oppress anyone..." (Lev.19:13).

In your own words say something like, *"Thou shalt not steal is the eight commandment God gave to Moses and unto all generations. Stealing reveals a lack of faith in God to provide. As little children depend and trust in their parents to provide them with food, shelter, and clothing, our heavenly Father wants us to trust and depend on him* (Matt.6.25-34; 7:11).

The word of God also declares, "**If you are a thief, STOP STEALING. Began using your hands for honest work, and then give generously to others in need"** (Eph.4: 28 NLB). *Demonic spirit of thievery I "bind" your suggestions to steal (Matt.16:19). It insults God, who is my heavenly Father and provider. From now on I will seek honest work in order to earn the money I need to purchase that which I desire. And if I can't find suitable work, the same God that provided for Elijah and the children of Israel will also make a way for me. In Jesus' name. Amen".*

7

BEWARE OF DEVICES THAT TRIGGER URGES TO USE

There are many gadgets and device used to smoke crack cocaine and the devil is extremely cunning in this particular area when it comes to tripping his victims up. Often the recovering individual is innocent of any serious contemplation of using, nevertheless, without fare warning they always seem to STUMPLE upon some form of paraphernalia or gadget use to smoke crack.

Since Ephesians 6:12, tells us that our war is *"against ...the UNSEEN world...and against wicked spirits in the heavenly realms"* (NLB), it's obvious that these doohickey used to smoke crack are strategically place in your path by the one who is waging this war against you. Satan.

His methodical approach of deception is the same course of action he used when he *"borrowed the serpent body"* (Gen.3: 1-4). He simply needed a physical presence to mastermind his plan. When God sent Jesus to earth He realized that Jesus would need to take on a physical presence in order to relate to us. **"So when Christ came into the world, he said, "You didn't want sacrifices and offerings, INSTEAD, YOU PREPARED A BODY FOR ME"** (Heb.10:5 NIV).

SATAN NEEDS A HOST TO USE BEFORE HE CAN LAY HIS TRAPS.

Since Satan *"was not blessed with a human body"* (see 1Cor.15:44) to maneuver around in the world he has to, by demonic principles *"possess"* (Matt 8:28, 31; Acts 8:7; 16:16) a human being—in this case other struggling addicts—in order to engineer the act distributing drugs, or make sure drug that some form of paraphernalia will be placed where it will be stumbled across.

Satan's intent is to **TRIGGER** the urge to use. These *"triggers," crack pipes,* are most often left behind or lost by some poor possess soul, who is not aware that he or she is being use as a "courier" by Satan, with the objective of tempting those who are struggling to be free.

PARAPHERNALIA USED TO SMOKE CRACK COMES IN MANY DISGUISES.

The apparatuses used to smoke crack come in many disguises. They comes in the form of carefully constructed aluminum cans with small pinholes fashioned in the center, a glass stem, copper tube, radio or television antenna compacted with copper wiring which serves as a screen in order to smoke crack. **Beware Of These Specific Triggers**

Those are just a few and since these objects are *visible* to the eyes they are called **VISUAL TRIGGERS.**

There's also another dimension of generates which I call **SENSE TRIGGERS** because they play tricks with the senses. Such as the constant flickering sound of a cigarette lighter, the smell of matches after the flame goes out, the distinct crumbling sound of an aluminum can, the taste of medicine with codeine, the conversing about past times when you once used, or even overhearing a conversation relating to using.

83

There are many other approaches that the enemy will try to use to arouse your interest because he knows your past, and he knows the struggles that you have had with past issues. In any event, if you unfortunately stumble upon any of these items IMMEDIATELY look away, and then respond, *"It is written…"*

POWER PRAYER

"Look not upon the wine when it is red, when it giveth his colour in the cup, when it moveth itself alright. At the last it biteth like a serpent, and stingeth like an adder" (Pro.23: 31-32).

Before we go any further let me give you a better understanding of what the writer is insinuating so that the verse will illuminate more power. When the writer said, *"look not thou upon the wine…"* he refers not only to that of wine, but all forms of chemical dependency or anything else that may obstruct you spiritual walk by arousing temptation. It doesn't matter if it's liquefied, solid, powder form; metal, aluminum, or whatever the matrix. **"Look not!"** Turn your attention IMEDIATELY away from it!

TURN YOUR ATTENTION SPAN IMMEDIATELY AWAY FROM THE DISTRACTION!

Now, after quoting Pro.23: 31-32, ***say in your own words something like:*** *Demonic spirit of deception, I rebuke you and the suggestion to linger in glance upon the object. The Holy Spirit has made me aware of your tactics, Satan. I know better now than to dwell on any such circumstances, because by doing so is like walking unexpectedly upon a cobra. And as a snake lies waiting in the bush to strike a poisonous blow, so is the purpose of any paraphernalia one stumbles upon or is introduced to, "it biteth like a serpent, and stingeth like an adder."*

84

Thank you Lord for making me aware of what the enemy is trying to accomplish by having these inventions strategically placed along my path. From this day on I will remember to immediately look away and walk away. Praise the Lord!

Option

"Touch not; taste not; handle not; which are all to perish with the using" (Col.2: 21-22).

THERE'S A REASON WHY YOU SHOULD BEWARE OF TOUCHING CERTAIN OBJECTS.

Before we get into reciting the second optional verse I want you to first understand the spiritual phenomenon behind *touching* certain items. Why? Because somewhere along the path of recovery and rededication to the Lord, you will come across some form of paraphernalia or possibly the drug itself and be tempted to touch the item. Maybe you simply want to discard of it, or out of curiosity to examine it authenticity.

Whatever the case, do not fall victim to such ignorance. **Touch not; taste not; handle not!** By simply *touching* certain objects a person can be subjected to the spirit—demonic or anointed—that it is associated with. Especially if the devil knows that particular object can be used to cause one of God's children to stumble or fall.

Stop Judging Your Misfortunes From Only The Natural Point Of View

I know you think the statement of simply by touching certain object can be detrimental sounds foolish, but that's exactly the way Satan wants you to think. He wants you to think with the **"natural mind and declare such spiritual, Godly information as foolish"** (1Cor2: 14). He doesn't want you come to a place in your life where

85

you'll finally begin to understand this spiritual war we're in (see Rev.12: 17).

Satan wants you to continue judging everything that happens in your life based on human wisdom. He doesn't want you to surrender to the wisdom *"which the Holy Ghost teacheth;* **comparing spiritual thing with spiritual"** (1Cor.2: 13).

Satan knows that as long as he can keep a person in a *"natural state of mind"* that when it comes to understanding the spiritual phenomenon's concerning the trials of life such conversation and acceptation would seem **"foolish to them"** (1Cor.2: 14b), because they have not developed a personal relationship with God, *"in order that he might reveal to them by his Spirit…the deep thing of God"* (see 1Cor2: 10-12).

Lack Of Spiritual Awareness Is Your Problem

The Word of God plainly tells us that we are to **"BE AWARE OF SATAN'S EVIL SCHEMES AND NOT TO BE OUT SMARTED BY THE DEVIL**" (SEE 2Cor.2:11 NLB). Distinctively speaking there is medical documentation and evidence of the skin's ability to absorbed certain medications and narcotics upon touch. Well, the same research applies to crack cocaine or the residue left upon the utensils used. Until a person comes to the conclusion that it's because of one of **"Satan's evil schemes"** (2Cor.2:11 NLB) that they're on drugs… this LACK OF KNOWLEDGE will keep them forever struggling under sin's power of ignorance.

My friend, don't allow yourself to remain *"natural minded"* when it comes to this spiritual war we are in. Open your mind to be educated by the Spirit of God and the Holy Ghost will teach you what the devil does not want you to know when it comes to *"comparing spiritual things with spiritual."* (See 1Cor.2:12-14).

86

According to the careful research, and the guidance of the Holy Spirit it has been revealed to me that by merely tasting, handling, or *"touching"* certain items a person can become spell bounded, or receive a miraculous healing depending on the spirit connected with the item. To confirm that, notice in Acts 19:12 that *"handkerchiefs and aprons"* were the instruments used to convey God's purpose.

The Apostle Paul simply *touched* the items and prayed over them. Afterwards the objects came into contact with certain individuals and **"they were healed, and any demons within them came out"** (Acts 19:12, LBV).

Dear Reader, please pay close attention. What I'm trying to get you to understand is that just as God was able to use Paul, and *aprons and handkerchiefs* as objects of purpose, Satan has the power to **"duplicate"** such a process by using items like crack-cocaine pipes, empty dope containers, and more.

BE ON YOUR GUARD, SATAN HAS THE POWER
TO DUPLICATE THE PROCESS BY USING CRACK
PIPES, EMPTY DOPE CONTAINERS, LIQUOR
BOTTLES, AND MORE.

Well, just in case you need more proof about **Satan's ability to incongruously duplicate certain feats,** notice in Exodus 7:8-11, that when Moses an Aaron presented themselves before the Pharaoh to display certain acts of God by casting down a walking stick, **"and it became a serpent" (vs.10),** that the Pharaoh called his sorcerers (operating under Satan's Power) **"and they also did IN LIKE MANNER with their enchantments" (vs.11).**

As you read on you will notice that each time Moses—who was operating under the anointing and power of God—performed an act, the Pharaoh's sorcerers—operating under the power of Satan—"**DID THE SAME BY THEIR SECRET ARTS**" (Ex.7:22 NRSV).

My point is that it doesn't matter if it's a walking stick, a piece of wood, cloth, glass, aluminum, or metal, depending on the spirit operating behind the initiative— God or Satan—there indeed will be a correlation.

Now I don't want to sound eccentric, but when it comes to this particular war (to be free of crack cocaine addiction) there are certain implements that recovering addicts and rededicating Christians must be conscious of before coming into contact with: Like all drugs and the paraphernalia used! These items are connected with evil, and release a diabolical spirit of persuasion when coming into contact with.

I, repeating the words of Timothy, reply, *"Think about what I am saying. The Lord will give you understanding in all these things"* (2 Tim.2: 7 NLB).

Again the medical reason you should not be so naive to handle such items is because the *RESIDUE* can be easily absorbed through the skin which will trigger an urge to use.

THE POWER PRAYER

M y friend, when you see a "crack-pipe", empty dope bag, or are approached by one of **"the children of the devil"** (1Jn.3: 10), who in this case would be a drug dealer or user, and they try to deceive you into utilizing any drugs or paraphernalia, IMMEDIATELY respond:

It is written **"Touch not; taste not; handle not; which are all to perish with the using"** (Col.2: 21-22).

Now say in your own words something like no! No! No! Not this time Satan. Yes, I was once ignorant of this paradox. I was blind, but now I see. Never again will I be deceived into touching, tasting, nor handling merchandise or oddments connected with spiritual downfall. I'm not so naïve that I think everything that I touch could result in evil consequences, but I now understand that when it comes to drugs or the paraphernalia used there is according to 2Chr. 18:20 an **"evil spirit of enticement"** *connected with it.*

If that's not true then why are so many people under the spell of these oddments, which some have made their god (Ex.20: 3; 32:1-4). Satan, I am "no longer ignorant of your devices" (2Cor.2: 11). I'm on to you. I know better now. Thank you, Jesus Christ. Amen.

Option

It is written, **"...touch not the unclean thing"** (2Cor.6: 17)

Now in your own words say something like: I will never be deceived again into touching anything that is considered unholy or unclean in the eyes of God. The Holy Spirit has now revealed to me that by touching anything that has an evil connection, or satanic motive, a door will be opened for the enemy to sway my conscience.

Satan, your product, crack-cocaine, and the implements used to smoke it are unholy and unclean. The product is toxic, the inventions used or shared are contaminated with residue, the germs and diseases of others, and using them is a sin against my body, which is the dwelling place of the Holy Spirit (1Cor.3: 16).

Just as a loving mother will not subject its fetus to anything toxic, I will no longer subject the Holy Spirit, who is like a spiritual fetus growing on the inside of me (see1Cor.6: 19) to anything unhealthy and unclean.

Thank you, Jesus. My eyes have been open to the truth concerning spiritual knowledge of the elements, and their connection with sanctity or evil. Praise the Lord!

8

APPLYING THE BLOOD OF JESUS TO STOP SATAN'S MEDDLINGS

"How much more, then, will the blood of Christ, who through the eternal Spirit offered himself unblemished to God, cleanse our consciences from acts that lead to death, so that we may serve the living God!" (Heb.9:14).

A lot of people go to church and hear sermons and sing songs about the blood of Christ but when it comes to their deliverance and protection they don't understand the significance and power of the blood of Jesus or how to apply it to their circumstances. The first recording we get concerning God using a blood is in Genesis 3:21 where God sacrifice an animal for the sin of Adam and Eve, and ever since then man a blood sacrifice has been required. (See Ex.24:8; 30:10; Lev. 17:11). None of us can enter into God's presence here or his glorious presence hereafter, *but through the blood of Jesus! Christ,* who is called *"the lamb of God"* (Jn.1:29, 36) became a more excellent sacrifice than the blood of calves and goats. Before we as ministers or Christians intercede for others we must first apply the blood of Jesus to ourselves for pardon and then pray for the errors of those we intercede or pray for. (See Lev.1:5; 4:1-7, 13-22; Num.15:22-31; Heb.9:7). The value of the life is the measure of the value of the blood. This gives the blood of Christ its inconceivable worth according to Hebrews 9:14. This gives the blood of Christ it's inconceivable **"voice"** and worth according to Hebrews 9:14.

CHRIST'S BLOOD HAS A VOICE!

Notice in Genesis 4:8-10 after Cain killed his brother Abel God asked Cain where his brother was but Cain pretended not to know. God responded, ***"The Voice of your brother's BLOOD crieth to me from the ground"*** (v 10). Abel's blood was both witness and prosecutor, before God's own knowledge. The blood is said "to have cried from the ground, the earth". Not only did Abel's blood cry out but his blood intercede for of all those who would have descended from him!

Well, the same way that Abel's blood cried out to God on his behalf and in the interest of all his potential descendants **"THE BLOOD of Jesus speaks louder and better thing that that of Abel's"** according to Hebrews 12:24. When Christ's was sentenced to death on the cross one of the soldiers took a spear, stuck him in his side and "the blood of Christ hit the ground" (Jn.19:34), Christ's blood spoke from the ground to God in our interest and in the interest of our children and their children, and their children's children saying, "Father, keep an eye on, protect, forgive, deliver, set free, bless, restore, and heal "say your name here" .

My friend, we wouldn't even be able to enter into God's presence kneel down and pray for those we love or the church if it were not for the forgiving blood of Jesus which *"apologizes for our ignorance sins and shortcoming"* (See Lev.4:1-6,13-17; Heb. 10:3,8-11; 19-22). The blood of Jesus *speaks to God on behalf of sinners; it pleads not for vengeance, but for God to have mercy on us*. It *speaks* pardon for our sins, and peace for our souls! The blood of Christ *speaks redemption* (1Pet.1:18-19) *not only from eternal misery hereafter, but from living a worthless life in this world* (Heb. 9:14). Christ's *blood justifies, presents us as righteous, witnesses and testifies* unto God supporting the truth concerning our Christian walk and faith.

"And Jesus Christ was revealed as God's own Son by his baptism in the water and by SHEDDING HIS BLOOD. And the Holy Spirit also gives us *testimony* that this is true. So we have three witnesses--the holy Spirit, the water, AND THE BLOOD..." (1Jn.5:6-8 NLT).

Now, in contrast to the ritual works of the old covenant, we are told about the superior ministry of Christ: **"When Christ came as high priest of the good things that are already here, he went through the greater and more perfect tabernacle that is not man-made, that is to say, not a part of this creation"** (Heb.9:11). The better blessings have already begun, the author reminds us. We already have forgiveness and direct access to God, because Christ went through the heavenly holy place.

Jesus Christ entered the reality, not the imitation, and he did it by a better sacrifice: "He did not enter by means of the blood of goats and calves; but he entered the

Most Holy Place once for all by his own blood, having obtained eternal redemption" (Heb. 9:12).

By dying for us, the Son of God was able to redeem us once for all. It was a perfect, sinless sacrifice, presented in the heavenly holy place, fully effective, never needing to be done again. This was a sharp contrast with the Levitical rituals, which were repeated continually yet never bringing the people any closer to God.

"The blood of goats and bulls and the ashes of a heifer sprinkled on those who are ceremonially unclean sanctify them so that they are outwardly clean" (Heb. 9:13; see Num.19:1-22).

Here the author refers to the ashes of a heifer. Like the other rituals, it had obscure details that had nothing to do with a person's conscience. Of course, Christ is much better than a heifer, and we should expect that his sacrifice achieves a much better kind of cleansing. **"How much more, then, will the blood of Christ, who through the eternal Spirit offered himself unblemished to God, cleanse our consciences from acts that lead to death, so that we may serve the living God!"** (9:14).

He offered a perfect sacrifice, willingly, and through faith in him, this cleanses us on the inside and enables us to worship God. We can do what the high priest could only symbolize: we can approach God with total confidence. We have been washed and purified by the blood of Christ — all sins are removed. If a burned-up heifer could ritually cleanse an Israelite, we can be sure that the sacrifice of Jesus is more than enough for us. Since Christ brings us complete forgiveness, he "is the mediator of a new covenant" (9:15). He gives us a relationship with God on a completely new basis — not the old covenant, but the new. And the result is "that those who are called may receive the promised eternal inheritance." This was achieved, the author reminds us, because "he has died as a ransom to set them free from the sins committed under the first covenant." Under the first covenant, many external regulations defined sin. Christ set us free from that. He forgives any kind of sin, but he sets us free from the rituals that were so important under the old covenant.

Without a doubt, the blood of Jesus Christ, the blood of the Son of God is the most precious gift God has given to His church!

Without a doubt, the blood of Jesus Christ is the most precious gift God has given to His church! Nevertheless, a lot of Christians today still don't understand the importance and power of **"the voice of the blood of Jesus"**. I've been studying on the importance of pleading the precious Blood of the Lord Jesus Christ to overcome the enemy, to protect ourselves and our families and for the protection of our property and possessions. I want to share some of that knowledge with you because we all need protection against Satan and his demons.

There is so much power in the Blood of the Lord Jesus Christ! By pleading the Blood of Jesus over your property, possessions, and family, you can put worry to rest all and any attacks from the enemy. The devil wants to rob us of salvation, deliverance, children, happiness, marriages, by making us think that we are up under some kind of curse but the truth is that we have been redeemed (rescued) from the curse of the law through the **Blood of the Lord Jesus Christ.** (See Gal.3:13; 4:4-5; 1Pet.1:18; Rev.5:9).

Revelation 12:11 tells us, **"And they overcame him (Satan) by the blood of the Lamb and by the word of their testimony."** Satan and his demons are out to destroy us but we can defend ourselves, our families and our possessions with the precious Blood of the Lord Jesus Christ! We have victory over evil and attacks of the enemy because Jesus shed His blood on the cross. Remember, the devil **was defeated** at the cross. Luke 10:19 confirms *"...I have given you authority over all the power of the enemy..."*

My friend, it time you begin to use that authority! Use the Blood of the Lord Jesus Christ against the enemy! **There must be a personal application of the blood of Christ in order to stem the tide of spiritual destruction in the life of the child of God... It is a personal matter. "The blood shall be to you for a token. When I see the blood, I will pass over you" (Exodus 12:13).**

The blood, **applied** by sprinkling, was all that was required for peace of mind and rest of heart. It took away all fear of the destroying angel. It was not mere interest in the blood, nor belief in its power; nor appreciation of its worth that availed. **It was the *applied blood* that counted.** Truth was translated into action. So it is with the blood of the Lord Jesus. **It is effective against satanic floods when applied by faith.** Too many Christians are living defeated lives with no real joy, peace, or power in their lives. Storm cloud after storm cloud keeps coming after them beating them down to a pulp. Many Christians, since they have not been properly taught how to apply, plead the Blood of Christ when they are faced with adversity are drowning in their sea of troubles. Just as priests applied the blood in the old covenant, we under the new covenant are to apply the blood of Jesus. *This is the blood of the testament which God hath enjoined unto you.* (Heb 9:20).

The word enjoined means to be given charge of. In the old covenant the priest applied the blood of animals by sprinkling. **In the new covenant we receive the blood by faith and sprinkle the blood with our words.** *"For with the heart one believes unto righteousness, and **with the mouth** confession is made unto salvation."* (Romans 10:10.) You apply the blood of Jesus to yourself **when you say,** "the blood of Jesus which He shed on the cross was for me, and it makes me free from sin and all unrighteousness."

Overcoming is a continual process in this life. **Whatever we apply the blood of Jesus to Satan cannot touch!** Whatever we apply the blood to becomes redeemed by Christ, it becomes His. Whatever we apply the blood to is made Holy. When the blood is applied so also is God's grace and the anointing of the Holy Spirit applied. The number one reason why so many

Christians are coming under such heavy attacks from both demons as well as evil people in this world is because they do not understand the Protection that the Blood of Jesus offers and therefore they don't have God's full protection on them, their love ones, or their possessions. And one of the reason they don't have God's full protection on them is because they have never been taught how to spiritually defend themselves using actual spiritual warfare techniques such as *the Pleading of The Blood Of Jesus!*

Christians can either choose to remain passive with their heads stuck in the sand, hoping that neither they nor any of their close loved ones will ever come under any kind of direct human or demonic attack – or they can choose to learn how to rise up in the power of their Lord and Savior Jesus Christ, and learn how to spiritually defend themselves using spiritual warfare techniques as given to us out of the Bible. When the enemy does come, and he will come at each one of us from time to time, you can either choose to run and hide hoping that you will somehow survive the attack and make it out in one piece – or you can choose to learn how to spiritually defend yourself and engage with the enemy.

Who And What Can I Plead The Blood On

The first thing you are going to want to do is make a PERSONAL list of everything that you would like to have God's protection on. Some of the basics are: your salvation, deliverance, body, soul, spirit, house, car, finances, job, spouse, children, ministry, and business. You will have to add your own personal things to the list to make it complete. Only God knows when any attack will be coming your way, and only God can protect you before these attacks occur. And the best way that you can get God to get involved with his full, divine protection is by pleading the Blood of Jesus on each of the specific things you want protected.

So how do you apply the Blood of the Lord Jesus Christ to your situation? By faith! In prayer and in faith you can plead the Blood of the Lord Jesus Christ over you and your family, your home, (demonic attacks against people in their homes have been completely stopped by applying the Blood of Jesus throughout the home - doors, windows, etc.).

You can draw a blood line of protection around your property, your vehicles, your children's schools, and your workplace with the precious Blood of the Lord Jesus Christ. **Remember, the devil cannot penetrate the house, ground, soul, or heart where the blood has been applied.**

Prayer

"Father, I plead the Blood over inch of my physical body, soul, and spirit. I plead the Blood over any diseases, viruses, and sicknesses that could possibly come against me. I plead the Blood over my marriage, children, finances, car, employment, tithes, and my neighborhood. Father, I apply and plead the Blood of Jesus against any demons, as well as against any evil people who try to come against me.

Thank you, Father for the precious Blood of the Lord Jesus Christ. Thank you that there is power in the blood, there is salvation in the blood and there is protection in the Blood of the Lord Jesus Christ from the deception of Satan and his demons. I am redeemed out of the hand of the

Father, I apply the Blood of the Lord Jesus Christ to my eyes, to cleanse them of any defilement, wickedness, or garbage I have watched that is not of You. I apply the Blood of the Lord Jesus Christ to my ears; to cleanse my ears of any defilement, wickedness, garbage, gossip or slander that I have listened to, so that I might hear clearly what the Lord is saying to me. I apply the Blood of the Lord Jesus Christ to my lips and to my tongue, so that You, Lord, will be able to cleanse me of those things that I have spoken that really haven't been of You at all.

Father, I apply the Blood of the Lord Jesus Christ to my heart and my mind. Since my heart is the creation center of the soul that produces all the emotions and thoughts, I ask You, Lord, to put the Blood of the Lord Jesus Christ on my heart, my thoughts, my emotions and cleanse my mind so that I may serve You. Father, I apply the Blood of the Lord Jesus Christ to my feet. Cleanse me from the corruption of this world.

Thank you, Father, for the power and authority that you've given me through the Blood of Jesus to stop all and any attacks form the enemy who tries to invade and steal my peace. I now have full faith and belief that the Power of The Blood of Jesus Christ will now protect me against the things that I have just pled His blood upon. Thank you Father, Thank You Jesus. Amen."

Praise God For The Power Of The Blood

"You were redeemed...with the precious blood of Christ..." (1 Peter 1:18-19 NIV).

The story of redemption begins in Eden with God shedding the blood of a lamb to cover Adam's and Eve's sin, and ends in heaven with a multi-national choir singing, *"...You...have redeemed us to God by Your blood out of every...nation."* (Rev. 5:9 NKJV). **We simply do not comprehend the great significance of the blood.** If I were to ask you what the power of the blood means, you might answer, *"It means that my sins are remitted—that I'm free from the bondage of iniquity—that all my sins are covered."* Yet, beyond forgiveness, what does the blood of Jesus Christ mean to you? Can you explain to me, to your family, to a coworker the value and virtue of the blood of Jesus? **I want to give you a fuller understanding of the preciousness of Jesus' blood—and how it can work wonderful changes in your life!** Most Christians know about the blood Jesus shed for us. When Christ lifted the cup at the last Passover, He said, "**...This cup is the new testament in my blood, which is shed for you**" (Luke 22:20).

We memorialize His sacrifice every time we have communion. But that is the limit of most Christians' knowledge of Jesus' blood. We know only about the blood being shed--**and not about it being sprinkled! Being pled over the attacks of the enemy!** The first biblical reference to the sprinkling of blood is in

Exodus 12:22. The Israelites were commanded to take a bunch of hyssop, dip it in the blood of a slain lamb, and sprinkle it onto the lintel and two side-posts of their front door. That night, when the death angel came and saw the blood on the door posts, he would pass over the house.

Please understand -- as long as the blood was left in the basin, it was of no effect; it was merely blood that had been shed. The blood had power to save only when it was lifted out of the basin and sprinkled! Why couldn't the Israelites have simply laid the basin of blood at the threshold and said, "It doesn't matter what we do with it. After all, blood is blood"? Suppose they had put the basin on a linen-covered table, or on a pedestal just inside the door? **I'll tell you what would have happened: The death angel would have struck that home! The blood had to be lifted out of the basin and sprinkled on the door to fulfill its purpose of protection.**

This blood in Exodus 12 is a type of the blood of Christ. The blood that flowed at Calvary was not wasted — it did not fall to the ground and disappear. No, that precious blood was collected in a heavenly fountain. **If Christ is Lord of your life, then your door posts—your heart—has been sprinkled by His blood.** And this sprinkling is not for forgiveness only -- **but also for protection! When you are sprinkled, you are totally under the protection of Christ's blood, against all the destroying powers of Satan. When his forces see Christ's blood on your door posts, they must pass over you. They cannot touch you – because they cannot touch anyone sprinkled with Christ's blood!**

So, you see, the preciousness of the blood has to do with much more than forgiveness. Jesus' blood has not been left in the basin -- but has been lifted out and sprinkled on your heart. And it is waiting to be sprinkled on the door posts of hearts around the world! Beloved, today we are in a new covenant with Jesus Christ -- a covenant sealed by His own blood. And likewise today, when His precious blood is sprinkled on your soul, it is for purposes of communion. It is so that you can go boldly -- with ease, without fear of judgment -- into God's presence for communion. You are given access to Him, with no sin condemning you. **If you want to overcome the devil, declare and stand on the blood!**

The blood of Jesus protects and declares us righteous in the eyes of God. We are not righteous because we go to church, don't curse, smoke, lie still or cheat, try to do the right thing, saying the right thing or act a certain way, "**we are made righteous** in the eyes of God by the **atoning blood of Christ and what he accomplished!** No man can every beat his chest and say he is righteous according to how he lives because that would be "**boasting of oneself**" and a sin (Eph.2:9). You are righteous and I am righteous only by way of the **BLOOD** of Jesus Christ!

"**I do not frustrate the grace of God: for if righteousness comes by the law, then Christ is dead in vain" (Gal.2:21.)** "**There is none righteous**" (Rom.3:10.) **"Not by works of righteous which we have done, but according to his mercy...which he shed on us abundantly through Jesus Christ our Savior"** (Tit.3:5-6). **"For they being ignorant of God's righteousness, and** going about to establish their own righteousness, have not submitted themselves to the righteousness of God" (Rom.10:3.)

"For he (God) made him (Christ) to be sin for us, who knew no sin; that we might be mad the righteousness of God in him" (2Cor.5:21.) The Blood of atonement goes all the back to the day of our ancestors who used animal sacrifices (see Lev.1:1-5, 11; 3:1-17; 4:1-5, 13-35; Num.19:4), but our **atonement** and **protection** comes through the *Blood* of Jesus Christ. "Neither by the blood of goats and calves, **BUT BY HIS OWN BLOOD**...obtained eternal redemption for us" (Heb.9:14).

"And since we have been made right in God's sight by the blood of Christ" (Rom.5:9 NLT.) we should use the privilege of declaring the Power of His Blood over ourselves and our love ones for protection! Like our ancestors did, sprinkle, **Apply** some blood on yourself and on the one who is struggling with addiction or some other sin! Why, because, **"Under the old system, the blood of goats and bulls...could cleanse people's bodies (minds) from ritual defilement. Just think how much more the blood of Christ will purify our hearts from deeds that lead to death so we can worship the living God"** (Heb. 9:13 NLT.)

Dear reader, it is my sincere prayer, **"That the Blood of Christ purifies the heart of the one you're praying for so that they will cease from their evil, rebellious deeds, that the Blood of Christ will purge (flush) their conscience from dead works, so that they can begin to worship God". In the name of Jesus Christ**

103

(Acts 16: 18), and **by the Power of His Blood,** crack **cocaine bondage, let them go so that may worship, serve the living God!** (See Ex. 8:1, 20; 9:1; 6:1).

Say aloud: "Lord, God, I cover myself and everyone around me with the blood of Jesus. I cover all of the members of my family (state them by name) with the blood of Jesus. I cover my home, my land, my car, my finances, my job, my husband, my wife, my children, my family, my ministry, with the blood of Jesus. In the Name of Jesus Christ, by the power of His blood, I break off every power of the kingdom of darkness and cancel every argument in heaven that has established itself against the plans of God in my life and spoil every attack of the enemy. I call forth, in the name of Jesus, and by the power of the blood all of God's plans and purposes for my life, and my family. As for me and my house, we shall serve the Lord. Satan, the blood of Jesus is against you and you have no authority over my life! NO WEAPON FORMED AGAINST ME (OR MY FAMILY) SHALL PROSPER!" because the Blood, the Blood, the Blood has been applied!

9

PRAYERS TO REJECT THOUGHTS OF SAME SEX INTERACATIONS

When it comes to understanding the numerous desperate perspectives that crack cocaine puts a person in, openly admitted homosexual men, after determining an individual is weak will target and wait for the opportunity to bring into play, as bait, crack cocaine to persuade otherwise straight men into allowing certain degradable sexual acts to be performed on them simply for a meager hit of crack. Although the person that is being blackmail with crack cocaine feels tainted when approached they will, *due to the desperation for hit of crack cocaine, sometimes disregard the shame, lower their dignity and give in to suggestion of allowing the admitted* **"homosexual to perform oral sex on them or other disgusting acts"** (See Rom.1:21,26-32).

After the person that's being blackmailed, seduced into allowing this sexual act to be performed on them gives in, what they don't realize is that **"the DEMONS that the *sexual immoral*, OPENLY ADMITTED HOMOSEXUAL person possesses are unknowingly being TRANSFERRED to them"** (1Cor.6:15- 16), and *after the **transfer** the* *individual that was **blackmailed, coaxed** will give in much easier the next time to the suggestion of homosexual participation* because **they now** accommodate a *"demon spirit of perversion"* (Isa.19:14; Acts 13:10; Gal.1:7; Deu.32:5) as well as **"MANY OTHER DEMONS"** that the declared, openly admitted gay person picked up from gay men that slept with in the past. (See Matt.12:43-45).

The Word of God declares that this manipulation, homosexuality is provoked a *"the spirit of sexual perversion"* (Jugd.19:22 LBV).

But before we go deeper into this subject matter I want you to realize that if you are a participant in homosexuality and have questions concerning the subject that the devil do all he can to persuade you not to read further because he doesn't want you to discover the answer to your questions from God's own mouth, the Written Word. But instead he wants you to accept what society has to say about the reasons for homosexuality and simply leave it at that. It's what's known as, *"Being ignorant of God's righteousness, pushing the the truth away and creating your own righteousness without really caring about What God has to say about a certain matter"*. (Rom. 10:3).

But just as a good lawyer tells his clients always to read the fine print of a contract before signing it, as a minister of God's I'm telling you that you need to read the fine print of God's Word on this subject before signing the world's contract of permissible or not permissible. Remember, **"The wrath of God is being revealed from heaven against all the godlessness and wickedness of men <u>who suppress</u> (exclude from consciousness) <u>the truth</u> by their wickedness"** (Rom.1:18 NIV).

Speaking of **suppressing the truth** there was a game show that use to come on years ago called *"To Tell The Truth"* and the participants had to figure out who was lying and who was telling the truth. Well, homosexuality **"IS A GAME"** of salvation and fact that Satan is playing with people, who like Eve deep in their heart are questioning, *"What God hath said"* about homosexual relations. Dear reader, if you're going to play "To Tell The Truth" with Satan then you need to simply prepare yourself before becoming a participant.

The reason the **"God's enemy and man's, Satan"** (Matt.13:37-39) wants the person taking part in homosexual relationships to disregard reading, hearing or discovering the truth about their reason for *"same sex attraction"* is because *"he, who was with God during the beginning of the creation of the heavens, earth and especially man"* truly knows how God feels about the subject matter (See Ezek. 28:13-18; Isa. 12--15), thereby giving him the inside scoop and making him a mastermind of the obliquity.

Very Careful Consideration Is Taken When It Comes To The Making And Drafting Of A Homosexual

When it comes to the making and targeting one for homosexual involvement Satan will use *"already committed homosexuals and lesbians as bait"* to sway the minds of the naive and innocent. (See Rom.1:32.) To add to the gay community he concentrates mainly on the young at heart, the slow to discern, the ignorant of God's word, a male child who was forced to take on the role of a female to help with younger sisters and brothers, a male child growing up without a positive father figure in his life and the mother condones the effeminate behavior, a child growing up under the influence of those who say it's okay to be gay but not verifying it with the Written Word Of God; the battered wife, the remorseful husband, **the homeless and the crack cocaine addicted.**

Why does Satan focus on the crack addicted you ask? It's because he knows that due to their adversity, the overwhelming cravings, weakness and despondency that some crack addicts struggle with that there's a good chance that their desperation will potentially play a part in them giving in to the suggestion of possibly allowing a gay man woman to fondle them or perform oral sex on them just so that they can get a hit of crack. And in many case this desperation for crack or money to buy crack has led many a straight man or woman into obtaining a steady homosexual relationship all for the purpose of getting crack cocaine as a reward. How can something like this happen to a straight man or woman? Because it was all well planned by *"the craftiest, cleverest, strategic, intelligent of all the creatures the Lord God had made, Satan"* (Gen.3:1 LBV), the master of *"the art of deception"* (Rev. 12:9; 13:14; 20:10).

Notice in Job 1: 6-8 that when God asked Satan **"where had he been and what had he been up to"**, Satan replied, **"I have been going back and forth across the earth, watching everything that going on"** (NLT). That verse alone proves two things. First, that when it comes to misfortune, or in the this case the introducing of drug to a person with leads to their addiction that the person didn't just happen go down the wrong road or run into the wrong people, but that Satan, *"who has been watching them very closely"* laid out a strategic plan for them to meet and befriend people who would introduce them to drugs and other misfortunes along the road of life.

The second thing that Job 1:7 proves is that just as Satan had been watching Eve and discovered that she could be easily deceived, manipulated, and that *"the word that God spoke to her could be corrupted"* (see Gen.3:1-6, 13), Satan knows by carefully studying the lives of certain people which individual or group to target when it comes to *"twisting God's word"* (Gen.3:1-2) and telling people one thing when God's word says another. There are a lot of verses in the that plainly tell us that homosexuality is **"unnatural"** and **"not God's will"** for any same sex couples to be intimate, but regardless many people are still walking around dumbfounded about how God feel about homosexuality.

What has happened to those who are lead to believe that God is okay with homosexuality and will overlook it as an abomination is that Satan, the same one who said to Eve, "did God really say that it would be a sin for you to you to eat of any fruit in the garden" (Gen.3:1, NLT) is still up to his old tricks and *deceiving people about what God word really says about sin!* He is still **twisting** the Written Word of God as well as the minds of people concerning the will of God in reference to homosexuality. And as a result a lot of homosexuals will say things like, *"I never read in the bible where God condemns homosexuality"* or, *"God is a forgiving God and he won't send anybody to hell for being in love with somebody"*.

My friend, what part of **"Do not have sexual relations with a man as one does with a woman; that is detestable"** (Lev.18:22), and **"Don't fool yourselves. Those who indulge in...homosexuality...will have no share in the kingdom of God"** (1Cor.6:9-10 NLT) don't you understand? And what part of **"And the men instead of having NORMAL SEX with women (which is God's will) burned with lust for each other and instead did SHAMEFUL THINGS with each other.."** don't you quite get!

The reason they can't get it is because ***"A demon spirit of sexual perversion and whoredom has possessed them"*** according to Hosea 4:12; 5:4 thereby causing them to "justify their homosexuality" and say things like they were born gay, but truth be told Ephesians 2:2 and 6:12 confirms that origin of the problem is because **"we are in a spiritual war against demons spirits that *provoke* and *influence* us to sin in different ways!"** And besides no one can be born gay because *"God is not the author of confusion"*(?), or in plain words, "since He was not in a confused state of mind when made man then it's evident that no person can be born gay or confused about their sexuality! Homosexuality is spiritual provoked by Satan, the spirit at work in the hearts of those who refuse to obey God" (Eph. 2:2 NLT).

110

What is a spirit? A spirit is simply a character trait influenced either by *"God, the Holy Spirit"* (see Gal.5:16, 22-25) or the *"influence and character traits"* of the devil (see Rev.13:6 CEV, 1Chr.21:1; Lk.22:3-6; Acts 5:3; Lk. 13:10). It's one reason why Jesus said to some, **"FOR YOU ARE THE CHILDREN OF YOUR FATHER THE DEVIL, AND YOU LOVE TO DO THE EVIL THINGS HE DOES...WHEN HE LIES (AND COMMITS OTHER SINS) IT'S CONSISTENT WITH HIS CHARACTER!"** (Jn. 8:44 NLT.)

Are Homosexuals The Product Of Evil Influence

From the very beginning when God created man and placed him in the Garden of Eden man *"the evils spirit of Satan's was masquerading around in the borrowed, possessed body of a serpent"* (Ge.:3:1), and so there is our first bit of truth concerning Satan, the evil spirit character's ability to possess the body of another and use it as an instrument to promote sin. And as man began to populate the earth's scene "Satan moved from the instrument of the serpent to the body of man, Cain and influenced him to not only show disrespect towards God, but to also kill his brother Abel out of jealousy! (Gen.4:1-8). It was that point on that *"the evil spirit of Satan's, the mighty prince of the power of the air, the spirit which is at work in the hearts of those who refuse to obey God"* (Eph.2:2) targeted Cain (Job 1:7; 2:2), his family (Gen.13-24) and other members of the human race to with the intent of possessing and using them to corrupt others

111

weak in the faith. It was only after years and years later that Adam and Eve gave birth to their son Seth **"that men began to once again worship, to distinguish themselves and call upon the name of the Lord"** (Gen.4:25-26). Nevertheless, it did not stop Satan, but gave him more opportunities to possess and hide himself in the crowd of human beings.

And as the human population began to rapidly grow on the earth the supernatural beings (corrupt angels) began to lust after, have sex with the human women and had children by them. This infuriated God, "made him sorry that he had made man" (Gen.6:6) and it was then that he decide to destroy that PERVERTED generation. (Gen.6:1-7). However, **"Noah found grace in God's eyes and God spared him, his wife, his sons and his daughters-in-laws"** (Gen.6:8-18) *"for the purpose of replenishing, repopulating the earth"* (Gen.10:32).

The problem was that although God killed, destroyed the PERVERTED human generation, there was no way to kill a spirit being and so they waited in the atmosphere for their chance to once again possess, hide themselves among the crowd of human beings *"masquerading as children of God"* (2Cor.11:13-15) *"until two of God's angels exposed them in Genesis 19:1-5, operating in the bodies of men who were being INFLUENCED to want to have sex with other men!"*

All throughout the beginning of the bible up to the new testament we find strong biblical evidence of **"perverted evil spirits possessing people"** (see Matt. 4:24; 8:16,28; 9:32; Acts 16:16) and **"influencing them to sin in some way or another"** (see Acts 5:1-3, 8-11; 13:10; Jn.13:2,27; Eph.2:2), but when it comes to the "rebellious, demonic influencing of same sex relationships" all of sudden most people will acknowledge that *"there's a spirit that causes women and men to commit whoredom, and other sexual immoralities* (see Hos.4:12;14, 5:4) but turn a blind eye to the truth about the "demon spirits that committed and influence sexual perversion" (Gen 6:2).

They somehow think that that demonic possession does not apply to them, that it's just part of their nature to be attracted to same sex partners. What's even more ironic is that just as Satan manipulated, twisted the commands of God and "beguiled, deceived Eve" (Gen.3:13) into going against God's will (see Gen. 2:15-17; 3:1-6) he is again *beguiling people,* twisting the word of God and making them think God has changed his mind about the punishment that people participating in same sex relationships will suffer according to Jude 5-7 and genesis 19:1-28 and that he now approves of the act. The truth is that according to 1st Samuel 15:29; Zechariah 8:14-15 and Psalms 110:4, **"God has not and never will change his mind, his principles concerning same sex relationships!"** The devil, "the father of lies" (Jn.8:44) is to blame for such warped thinking!

113

Who Were The First To Practice Homosexuality

This exploitation, history, and origin of the *homosexuality encouragement* began with celestial beings ignoring God's spiritual laws not to counteract sexually with human women. However, they **choose** to disregard God's decree, and due to their depraved, **PERVERTED REASONING** the characteristics of their nefarious spirit multiplied, and continue to spread throughout our society **today.** I know it sounds farfetched but according to God's Word *perverse character* began with the fallen angels, "celestial spirits" that **"became PERVERTED IN THEIR THINKING"**, chose to have unnatural, unorthodox sexual relations with human women,** and as a result **PERVERTED, PROFANE, SACRILEGIOUS CHILDREN** were conceived.

The Bible confirms, "In those day, and even afterwards, **WHEN THE EVIL BEINGS FROM THE SPIRIT WORLD WERE SEXUALLY INVOLVED WITH HUMAN BEING they had children by them**..." (Gen. 6:4). Well, be it to some a surprise, that *"evil spirit and nature"* of *"the prince of* **THE POWER OF THE AIR,** *the spirit that encourages disobedience"* (Eph.2:2) still abides **IN THE ATMOSPHERE TODAY** "being reassigned" to *possess men and women as they did back then* (See 19:3-9; Dt.13:13-14; Judg.19:22-23) with the intent of inflicting *distorted* sexual preferences **JUST AS THEIR SEXUAL PREFERENCE WAS DISTORTED.** Remember, dear reader, **"our struggle is against persons without bodies...against** huge numbers of wicked spirits in the spirit world" (Eph.6:12 LBV), *"The spirit that is at work in* **THE HEARTS** *of those that rebel against God's Word"* (Eph.2:2 LBV).

The underlining factor is that just as *"the Holy Spirit of God was able to impregnate Mary"* (Matt.1:20; Lk.1:31, 34-35), *"these* evil spirits *were duplicating the act"* (Gen.6:4), but instead of producing *"children that were filled with the Holy Ghost from the womb"* (Lk.1:15) they were producing **"children filled with PERVERSION and disobedience FROM THE WOMB"** (Eph.2:2).

After **"God saw the extent of human wickedness due to being possessed by these perverted spirits he said, I will blot out...mankind that I created"** (Gen.6:5-7,11-13). **"But Noah found grace in God's eyes and so God decided to spare Noah and his family, but the flood wiped out the rest of mankind"** (Gen.6:17-22; 7:17,23).

Although God wiped out these people who were *"possessed by these spirits' of sexual perversion"* (Gen.6:5) **the evil spirit** maneuvered its way into an awaiting society and manifested itself again through the family tree of Shem, Ham, and Japheth, and lastly **"THE DEMON SPIRIT OF PERVERSION REVEALED ITSELF IN THE CHARACTER AND LIVES OF VARIOUS MEN AROUND SODOM AND GOMORRAH"** (Gen.18:20-23; 19:4-5).

This statement and proof of God's word clarifies that although a man may die, you can't kill a spirit. The spirit simply moves on *from one generation to the next,* as we see where their rebellious, perverted character again showed up in **"the sons of Belial"** (Judg.19:22). Ironically the spirits continues to manifest their perverted character in the lives of men today (Rom.1:26), although we are supposed to be a more enlighten society. *One Version of the Bible refers to men and women who desire same sex partners as* **people who are possessed by what is called "A EVIL SPIRIT OF SEXUAL PERVERSION"** (Judg.19:22 LBV). The best thing we can do, *"until God casts these rebellious angels spirits into the pit of hell for eternity"* (Rev. 12:12; 20:10) is to do or best to better understand their purpose, unmask and **"resist their enticements"** (Js.4:7).

SCENARIO:

Today happened to be your payday. You'd been hanging the crack house getting high the majority of the day, and unfortunately you've run out of money. All of a sudden a homosexual happens to approach you and make you an offer, or maybe you have been sitting at home and the *desperate* thought of allowing yourself to be fondled, prostituted by a member of the same sex simply to acquire drugs crossed your mind.

Whatever the case, **IMMEDIAYELY** rebuke the suggestion or thought and say to the demon:

POWER PAYER

The Word of God says "**...Be not deceived: neither** fornicators... nor adulterers, **NOR EFFEMINATE (HOMOSEXUALS)**...shall inherit the kingdom of God (**1Cor.6: 9, 10b NLT**).

Now in <u>your own words</u>, *say something like: Demon spirit of homosexuality/lesbianism I rebuke you in the name of Jesus! The Word of God plainly acknowledges that all those who participate in such activity will not inherit the kingdom of God. I understand now that the verse is referring to men or women "... who commit homosexual acts will not inherit the kingdom of God" (TBV).*

Thank you, Lord for pointing it out to me in the Word where I was being deceived. Yes, Satan even told me that You would overlook sins of homosexual involvement simply because you are a loving God. However, I've come to understand now that if you, God, judged and condemned the past nations of this abomination when they didn't repent, You will also judge and condemn today's unbelievers. Your word clearly says that, **Those cities were destroyed by fire AND CONTINUE TO BE A WARNING TO US that there is a hell in which sinners (homosexuals) are punished"** (Jude1: 5, 7 LBV).

Satan, you may have deceived and influenced the President, and Congress to rise above God's Word, change and create a legislature that supports gay rights, and gay marriages, but the God that I serve, and **"the truth, establishment of His Word will never change!"** (Ps.119:160;Mal.3:6). **Therefore, such relationships will always be an "abomination disgusting in his**

sight" (Lev.18:2-322, 27). *God didn't put up with the selfishness and ignorance back then and he's not going to put up with it today!*

Thank you, Lord, for forgiving me. Thank you for your grace, which has given me time to come to my senses and realize the error my ways. Thank you for putting me back on the right path and closing hell's door. Amen.

Option

It is written, **"Thou shalt not lie with mankind, as with womankind: it is an ABOMINATION"** (Lev.18: 22). **"Do not lie with a man as one lies with a woman; that is DESTABLE"** (Lev.18:22 NIV).

Now in your own words, say something like: Demonic spirit of homosexuality or lesbianism, I rebuke you in the name of Jesus. I know what you're up to Satan. You 're trying to arouse a spirit of perverseness in me, hoping that I would go out and commit an abominable act of homosexuality/lesbianism simply to get drugs. I know that you've been aware of my battle with crack-cocaine, but today I'm claiming deliverance in the name of Jesus!

Not only am I claiming deliverance from crack, but also from the nescience of your presence and diplomacy; from the stupidity of belittling myself to the point of allowing another of the same sex to take pleasure with me in order to receive drugs. According to Leviticus 18:22 I realize now that God detests a homosexual lifestyle. It is unholy, corrupted, disgusting, and unacceptable as a child created in the image of God.

118

*I cast down all **"satanic suggestions"** (see2Cor.10:
5) that attempt to exalt itself against the knowledge of
God. That also includes any suggestions that attempt to
justify homosexuality. In the name of Jesus I **"bind"** (see
Mk.3: 27) any cravings for crack cocaine that may be
attempting to surface. May the precious blood of the
Lamb of God, Jesus Christ, shield my mind and heart
from the flaming arrows and suggestions of the evil one.
May His blood wash away any thoughts of impurity, and
deliver me from any "presumptuous sins" (Ps.19: 13).*

*Thank you, Jesus. Thank you for "the power of the
blood which enables me to overcome" (Rev, 12:11a). In
your Holy and Precious name I pray. Amen.*

Option

It is written, **"If a man lie with mankind, as he
lieth with a woman, both of them have committed
an abomination: they shall surely be put to death"**
(Lev.20: 13).

**"The PENALTY for HOMOSEXUAL acts is death
to both parties. They have committed a detestable
act..."** (Lev.20: 13 NLB).

Now in your own words, <u>say something like:</u> *In the
name of Jesus Christ, I rebuke all demonic thoughts of
homosexuality/lesbianism. According to the Word of God
it is written that no man should lie with another man,
and no woman should lie with another woman. It is
detestable and **sickening** in the eyes of God. It is an
abomination. Which means it is **something that God
hates**. God is the same God today that he was when he*

119

gave the commandment of Leviticus 20:13 and all other commandments regarding homosexuality.

In today's world He does not allow death by stoning anymore. Yet, those who continue to practice such a detestable lifestyle might a well be stoned to death because the judgment they will receive *"in the lake which burns with fire and sulfur"* (Rev21: 8), "separating themselves from an eternal life with God" *(seeMatt.25: 31-33, 41; Rev.20: 15) will be even worse!*

The Bible plainly says that **the abominable (homosexuals, lesbians, fornicators, adulterers, whores and whoremongers...) shall have their part in the lake, which burneth with fire (Rev.21: 8).** *I rebuke the spirit of homosexual suggestion right now in the name of Jesus! I came into this world as a separate identity. And it is God's will, according to His Word* **"it is not acceptable for me to turn against God's natural plan and indulge in sex with a same sex partner"** (Rom.1:26-27 LBV).

Thank you dear, Lord, for restoring my sanity, for delivering me from the deception and ignorance of homosexual influence. Praise the Lord!

10

No More Confusion About Homosexuality

God did wake up one day and say, **"I think I'll make this one a man, no maybe a woman. I can't make up my mind so I guess I'll let them deal with the confusion and figure out who they want have sex with on her own".** It amazes me how people can pick out some things in the Bible and choose to accept such as heavenly prosperity, the privilege of prayer, divine healing...and ignore other topics such as eternal damnation, hell's guests, demonic possession, and being cursed, when everything in the Bible is the truth, especially concerning *"our war against evil influences"* (Eph.2:2; 6:12). Again, so that you won't be confused any longer, the institution of homosexuality is connected to the insertion, **"sons of God"** (Gen.6:2,4), who were actually, **"beings from the spirit world"** (Gen.6:2 LBV), **"fallen angels which kept not their first estate"** (Jude 6-7), or "**Nephilims"**, which is defined as **"THE OFFSPRING OF DAUGHTERS OF MEN BY DIVINE BEINGS"** (Harper's Bible Dictionary) is how sexual perversion enter society.

The *New Unger's Bible Dictionary* declares, **"THE NEPHILIMS** are considered to be *giant* **DEMIGODS** (a being who is partly divine and partly human),

THE UNNATURAL OFFSPRING OF "THE DAUGHTERS OF MEN" (mortal women) IN COHABITATION (an intimate relationship) WITH THE "SONS OF GOD" *(angels)*. IT WAS SUCH A <u>"SHOCKING ABNORMALITY"</u> THAT GOD HAD TO NECESSITATE THE WORLDWIDE JUDGMENT OF THE FLOOD! (See Gen.6:5-17, New Unger's Bible Dictionary Commentary).

Simply put, according to Genesis 6:2 and verse 4 when DEMON SPIRITS IN THE EARTH WERE LITERALLY raping AND IMPREGNATING THE WOMEN they were ironically, *diabolically* duplicating of the feat God preformed when *"He impregnated Mary by the Holy Spirit"* (Lk. 1:35). The difference is that when Satan, he produced the *"*Nephilims*",* and OFFSPRING OF CHILDREN BY DIVINE BEINGS", *giant* DEMIGODS (a being who is partly divine and partly human), AND THIS UNDETECTED REMNANT, OFFSPRING, AND CHARACTER OF THESE EVIL BEINGS is evident today in *the display* of perverted characteristics as is noted in Genesis 19:4-9.

God's word confirms that *homosexual exploitation* is indeed *instigated* by *"a* SPIRIT *of perversion"* (Jugd.19:22 LBV) that causes people of the same sex to *"perversely"* desire relations with each other. Although God's Written Word clearly tells us **"people who participate in acts of homosexuality will not enter heaven"** (1Cor.6:9), because regardless of their commitment to each other **"they know in their heart that that such relationship it's wrong because "THE TRUTH OF GOD IS KNOWN TO THEM INSTINCTIVELY AND THEY HAVE NO EXCUSE!**

(Rom.1:18-19 NLT). But regardless they give in to the suggestion participate in the sin **due to a lack of "uncompromising stern religious teaching"** (Ex.18:19-21) **"which should have of began at home at an early age"** Dt.6:7, 20-25; 4:5,9; Lev.10:10-11) **"about what God hates"** (Lev. 18:1-3, 20-22; 20:13; Dt.23:17-18; 1Cor.6:9).

When Stern Teachings Of God are Rejected Children Perish

And since the **stern teaching** of abominations are rejected in the home, and the government has allowed the sin same sex marriages young girls and boys grow up *confused* about their sexuality, how they are supposed to **"dress and act"** (Deu.22:5) and as a result they are left to the reasoning and view of a society **"that doesn't truly fear or know God".** (See Dt5:29; 4:10; Ps.36:1-4; 34:11; 119:63), **"...and the result is that their minds become dark and confused"** (Rom.1:21).

One of the things that I tell people to consider is that if they're confused about their sexuality all they have to do is read, acknowledge the sign of the restroom that they normally use when out and about, or simply look between their legs and conclude what God gave them. In other reasoning than that comes from **"THE DOCTRINE OF THE DEVIL"** (1Tim.4:1). Speaking of the doctrine, set of guidelines and **principles of the devil** many people have been deceived into believing that homosexuality is a fault or mishap at birth, but since **"God is not the author of confusion"** (1Cor.14:33) how can people conclude that God *confusingly* made a mistake **"while planning, creating** and nourishing them in their mother's womb" (See Ps.139:13-17).

Can A Person Be Born Gay

A lot of people when ask, *"What drew you to become active in homosexuality?"* will respond, *"I was born like this"* or give some other supposed answer, **but the truth, according to God's Word, is that the inventiveness to participate in "perverted HOMOSEXIAL ACTS" actually does stem from being influenced by an** "evil spirit character" that has possessed the individual.

When most people hear the word possessed used they automatically think of some ghostly television show, but when the Bible speaks of a person being possessed it is referring to what today's society calls cloning, taking the DNA forma human host, inserting it into a living cell to create the exact replica of the person. Well, **spiritual cloning** has been around since the beginning of time. It began with God and then Satan, *"being the smartest of all the angels"* (Gen. 3:1) learned how to *"duplicate the miracle and process"* as we see evident of ability to *duplicate* in Exodus 7: 11; 8:7, 18-19.

God Was The First To Apply Spiritual Cloning

When God said, *"Let us make man in our own image and likeness"* (Gen.1:26-27), the image is found chiefly in the fact that man is a personal, rational, and moral being. While God is infinite and man finite, nevertheless man **possesses** the elements of personality

124

similar to those of the Divine person. Man is according to 1st Thess.5:3 **a trinity, made up of body, soul, and spirit**; and because "God is a spirit" (J.4:24), man's tripartite nature is not to be confused with the original "image and likeness" of God which being spiritual. **Being created in God's image and likeness relates to the elements of personality.** On the other hand the elements, cloning, and spirit personality of Satan is also too reckoned with.

Once God said that He was going to create, instill is us *His elements of personality,* *"Satan, who wanting to be like God"* (Isa.14:13), *"after being expelled from heaven and now bitterness and angry with God"* (Rev 12:7-9, 17), said to himself, **"I'LL POSSESS, CLONE ME A MAN TOO"** (Matt.8:16, 28, 34; Acts 16:16), and I'll instill in him the elements of my own evil, corrupt, disobedient personality. (See Jn.8:44; Eph.2:2; Acts 5:3; Jn.13:2, 27).

My friend, to be *"created"* means that you were spiritually cloned, enhanced with the characteristics, personality of the Spirit of God according to Genesis 1:26-27 and 2:7. To be *"possessed"* means that a person's mind and body has been overtaken, *hijacked,* taken hostage, **violated by the personality, spirit and character** of Satan's according to Matthew 17:15-18, Mark 5:2-13, Acts 8:7 and Matthew 4:24.

What Happens When A *Perverted Spirit* Takes Over A Person's Soul

When an individual become *"possessed by an evil spirit of perversion"* **they take on THE SAME PERVERTED SPIRIT, CHARACTER AND THINKING** that the fallen angels displayed and went about to have "sex with human woman, which was a violation of God's for will for their lives". Well, the very same *"spirit of* **perverted thinking** *that overtook the sons of Belial"* and *COMPELLS THEM* to desire to have sex with other men (See Judg. 19:22 LBV), is still overtaken men and women today as the result is the same! **"Woman TURN AGAINST GOD'S NATURAL PLAN** and *feel compelled* to have sex with each other. And men **instead of having a normal sex relationship with woman** will burn with lust for each other and **DO SHAMEFUL THINGS** with each other" (Rom.1:26-27 LBV).

These "fallen angels", demonic spirits of confusion and perversion **AFTER TAKING POSSESSION,** manipulating, and manifesting itself the spirit **WILL CAUSE THE PERSON IT POSSESSES** to became *COMPELLED* overwhelmed, **PERVERTED IN THEIR THINKING** and desire to have sex with someone of the same sex. **THE SAME PERVERTED SPIRIT, CHARACTER AND THINKING** that the fallen angels displayed when they decided they were going to have PERVERTED SEX with human women! Simply, it's a perverted *character defect* in that all homosexuals wrestle with!

SATAN today STILL CONTINUES TO DECEIVE MILLIONS

These same "**sons of God**", "**fallen angels**", "**evil being form the spirit world**" (Gen.6:2,4) are now assign to new regions, and "**operating to in new bodies (Matt.12:43)** have quietly discreetly maneuvered their way into our society and the result is a **continual wide spread of their perverted, immoral character.**

It's demoralizing to think that even in a society as advanced, intellectual, and spiritual informed as ours is today that **Satan still continues to deceive millions into thinking that homosexuality and lesbianism is acceptable when the word of God clearly says:**

"**DON'T FOOL YOURSELVES** Those Who Indulge In Sexual Sin...**WHO ARE...HOMOSEXUALS**—Will Have No Share In His Kingdom" (1Cor.6: 9 NLB).

The Gospel truth is that *God does not today, nor has he ever approved* of such "**unnatural and shameful behavior**" (Rom.1:21 NLT). And nothing could be more enlightening than the example He made out of Sodom and Gomorrah: "Remember Sodom and Gomorrah, and the nearby towns, whose people...indulged in sexual immorality and perversion: **They suffered the**

Punishment Of Eternal Fire AS **A PLAIN WARNING TO ALL"** (Jude1: 7).

People Today Involved In Homosexual

Relationships Also Has Been Warned

"In the same way, Sodom and Gomorrah and neighboring towns practiced immoral sexual relations and pursued other sexual urges. By undergoing the punishment of eternal fire, **they serve as a warning"** (Jude 1:7 CEV), **for today's society and future generations!** The Word of God tells us that *homosexuality, and all other forms of sexuality immorality is a malicious "mind game of luring unstable souls"* (2Pet. 2:14 CEV) into ignorantly committing various sins.

JUST AS SATAN TRIED TO LURE JESUS, HE IS STILL USING AS BAIT THE LURE OF MONEY, POWER, POPULARITY, AND RECOGNITION (see Lk. 4:5-6) to get today's politicians *to do his dirty work of legalizing same sex wedding ceremony, and spousal benefits*. To add insult to injury Satan has people establishing churches for **unrepentant homosexuals** as he has convinced the leader and members of this influential society into preaching and believing that although the people of homosexual relationships were punished and condemned it he Bible, that the punishment was for those people of that era and not for today's society! The truth is that **"GOD HAS NO FAVORITES WHEN HE JUDGES"** (1Pet.1: 17 NLB), and **according to Malicah.3:5-6** "God's Word does not change" simply to please a certain group of people

128

when it comes to the judgment of sexual perversion. The truth is that "its people **"being ignorant of the righteousness that comes from God, and seeking to establish their own"** who have a tendency to try and change God's judgment concerning sin, NOT GOD! (See Pro.24:21-21; Rom. 10:3; Ezek.5:6). What it all boils down to is just another **"mind game"** of challenge the Word that Satan is playing with people to undermine **"What God really means and has to say about specific matters"** (Gen. 3: 1-6).

"Now the serpent was more *subtle* {deceitful} and crafty than any living creature of the field which the Lord God had made. *And he [Satan] said to the* woman, CAN IT REALLY BE THAT GOD HAS SAID..." (Gen.3:1 AMP).

Dear reader, how much **plainer does a warning have to be** before we as earthly children decide to stop deceiving ourselves into thinking and **accepting the devil's lie** that God is loving, forgiving, and that He will look over their disobedience of homosexuality? **"GOD HAS NO FAVORITES Who Can Get Away With Sin!"** (1Pet.1: 17 NLB). If God PUNISHED the people of Sodom and Gomorrah, where **"...men lust for other men, and those cities were destroyed...and their offense CONTINUE TO BE A WARNING TO US THAT THERE IS A HELL IN WHICH SINNERS ARE PUNISHED"** (Jude 1:7 TEV), then **God will also punish today's participants!** In order to avoid the punishment God commands all His children to examine the Written Word, and above all **"STUDY"** (2 Tim.2:15), and know the Word for yourself in order to keep from being deceived by the enemy. The world has been once again warned, yet some still choose to ignore this truth and go about **justifying their selfish, perverted ways.** The writer of Romans puts it another way by saying, "...**being ignorant of the righteousness (living a life pleasing to God) that comes from God, AND SEEKING TO ESTABLISH THEIR OWN RIGHTEOUSNESS,** They Have Not Submitted TO GOD'S RIGHTEOUSNESS** (Rom.10: 3 NRSV).

Why Some People Are Comfortable In Their Sins

When it concerns *justifying sin* or *being comfortable in sin* when a person has a **"reprobate mind"**, **all they will care about or want to do is please themselves!** They will refuse to acknowledge God by their lifestyle, and even after knowing the truth they continue to *willfully* sin. Such people don't fully understand that **"EVERY SIN HAS IN EITHER IGNORANCE OR THE HATRED OF GOD".** (See Rom. 1:28, Matthew Henry Bible Commentary). Since God will not force anyone respect and love Him, but instead gives us **"the gift of choice"** (Josh.24:15; Job 34:4), the *worst thing* that can happen to a person is **"for God to turn them over to a reprobate mind".** In other words, *for God to get out of their way, shut up, and let them do what they want to do"* (Rom.1:28), similar to what we tell people who try to warn us about sin when we say to them, **"Shut up. I don't want to hear or care about what**

130

you have to say. I'm going to do what I want to do. I know what I'm doing is a sin, so leave me alone!

The Bible adds, "They are fully AWARE OF GOD'S DEATH PENALTY for those who do these things, yet they go right ahead. **And, worse yet, they encourage others to do them, too"** (Rom.1: 32 NLB).

Do You Know Anyone Who Died A Homosexual And Didn't Repent

Please, do not get offended by what I'm about to say but it is the Biblical truth. And that is, if you knew of anyone who died a homosexual or lesbian, did not repent, and you have been led to believe they went to heaven, you have been deceived.

What part of **"DON'T FOOL YOURSELVES, THOSE WHO INDULGE IN SEXUAL SIN, THOSE... WHO ARE...HOMOSEXUALS...WILL NOT HAVE A SHARE IN THE KINGDOM OF GOD** (1Cor.6: 9-10 NLB) do you not understand?

And what part of, **"BUT COWARDS WHO TURN AWAY FROM ME... THE CORRUPT AND SEXUAL IMMORAL— THEIR DOOM IS IN THE LAKE THAT BURNS WITH FIRE AND SULFUR"** (Rev.21:8 NLT), and what portion of, **"SODOM AND GOMORRAH AND THEIR NEIGHBORING TOWNS, ALL FULL OF LUST OF EVERY KIND, INCLUDING LUST OF MEN FOR OTHER MEN. THOSE CITIES WERE DESTROYED...AND CONTINUE TO BE A WARNING TO** (Jude 7 LBV) do you not understand?

How PLAIN does it have to be before you stop accepting the devil's lie concerning God's will for your life when it comes to sexual relationships? My friend, It's only because *"of the grace of God"* (Jude 1:4), *"by way of Jesus Christ"* (Rom.3:23-24; 5:15, 19-20), that people who are deceived into participating in such tainted lives of homosexuality are given time **to change, to repent before dying** (Acts 3:19), otherwise they *too* would have be wiped out by God a long time ago (Gen.6:5-7).

It is by the **"grace"** (Jude1: 4) of God, and his *compassion "not willing that any should perish"* (2Pet.3: 9), **"DIE AND GO TO HELL"** (Matt.23:33; LK.16:23; Act2:31) that fornicators, adulterers**, homosexuals** and **lesbians** are given time to **"turn away from this evil sin"** (Rev.2:21-22; Acts 8:22 NIV). But if they *choose* to continue believing the devil's lie concerning **homosexuality and going right ahead** "establishing their own righteousness" (Rom10: 3) **they too will suffer** "as **Sodom and Gomorrah and the towns around them...gave themselves over to this sexual sin, homosexuality...which is the worst possible kind,** are set forth as an example suffering the vengeance of **ETERNAL FIRE** (Jude 1:7).

Please Go Back To God's Original Plan

Please, don't be like Abraham's sons in law and **"mock"** the person who's trying to warn you about sin" (see

Gen.19:14). I beg you stop letting the devil fill your head with silly ideas of what God is like and what he will tolerate! **Read God's Word and "Allow the truth of God's Word to cut deep into your innermost thoughts. To expose the devil's lies for what they really are"** (Heb.4: 12 NLB). **DO YOU THINK THAT GOD WOULD JUDGE AND CONDEMN THE PAST NATIONS OF THIS SIN AND OVERLOOK YOU WHEN YOU DO THEM, TOO?"** (Rom.1: 18, 21, 26, 27; 2:3 LBV).

Dear Reader, if the **"deceptive spirit"** (Rev.12: 9; 13:14; 20:10) of homosexuality or lesbianism is now or has ever influenced you to participate in such an unholy, abominable, disgusting act I beg you to confess you sin and **"REPENT** of this sexual sin that goes against God's **natural plan"** (Rom.1: 26 LBV).

Whether you want to believe what I'm about to say or not, the truth is that people who are **"suffering" from the disease of aids and those who "CONTRACTED IT THROUGH HOMOSEXUALITY"** the Bible confirm that their suffering is due to their twisted life style!

"Being **FILLED WITH SHAMEFUL LONGINGS... MEN TURNING AWAY FROM THE NATURAL LOVE FOR WOMEN. They burn with sexual longing for each other MEN DID SHAMEFUL THINGS WITH OTHER**, Women committed sexual acts with each other that were **NOT NATURAL. THEY SUFFERD IN THEIR BODIES FOR ALL THE TWISTED THINGS THY DID"** (Rom.1: 26-27 NIV).

On the other hand, *the infection of aids contracted any other way such as by a blood transfusion* is simply **"THE DEVIL'S WAY OF TRYING TO DESTROY GOD'S GOOD PEOPLE ALONG WITH THE WICKED"** according to Genesis 18:20-21, 23-33; 19:1-5,7,12-15,24-29.

Well What If I Simply Like Wearing Clothes Of The Opposite Sex

Before ending this chapter I would like to add something further just for those who might try to justify themselves and say, *"I'm not gay. I just like wearing clothes of the opposite sex"*, or *"I'm only a cross dresser and nothing more"*.

Well, my friend, the Word of God says that **"The woman shall not wear that which pertaineth to a man, neither shall a man put on a woman's garment; for all that do so are an abomination unto the Lord thy God"** (Dt. 22: 5).

Now, although that statement is clear there will still be some who try to argue the point by saying, *"Well, everybody knows that they make clothing that men and women wear alike. So, am I wrong or sinning if I wear unisex clothing?"*

The answer is, "Nothing's wrong with wearing unisex clothing such as blue jeans, t-shirts, baseball caps, or even construction pants and boots if require for a job, but let's be honest with the matter at hand because we all know that "God is merely addressing the issue of men who dress up like women and women who dress up like men with

134

the intent of appear to the public or their homosexual partner as something that their not!"

In most homosexual or lesbian relationships one person will dress up like a man and the other will dress up like a woman. This sinful, abominable, deceptive character is meant to make the one who dresses like a woman feel as though they are with a man and visa-versa. This sort of dress code and behavior is what God is addressing and despises!

11

Prayers To Negate Notions of Drinking Occasionally

*I*N this chapter we will discuss alcohol consumption in connection with the individual's recovery from *"crack"* cocaine addiction as well as the security of that person's salvation when alcohol is reintroduced into the equation. Since I've been in the ministry of counseling recovering addicts I've been often asked, *"Is it okay to take a drink every now and then, or on special occasions, now that I've conquered the crack cocaine struggle?"*

The answer, my friend, is no! Why? Because when a person is rebounding from crack addiction the demonic spirits of chemical influence are waiting for what the Bible refers to as the **"opportune moment"** (Lk.4:13 NIV) as in the case of Jesus' temptation in the wilderness. The following verse demonstrates:

"Then Jesus, full of and controlled by the Holy Spirit, returned from the Jordan and was led in [by] the [Holy] Spirit... For (during) forty days in the wilderness (desert), where He was tempted tried, tested exceedingly) by the devil. And He ate nothing during those days, and when they were completed, He was hungry... And when the devil had ended every [the complete cycle of] temptation, he [temporarily] left Him [that is, stood off from Him] until another more opportune and favorable time" (Lk.1, 2, 13 AMP).

"Be sober...because your adversary the devil...walketh about seeking whom he may devour" (1Pet.5:8).

My friend, the moment that you allow yourself to be **deceived into thinking you can handle drinking now** that you've overcome crack cocaine is the moment Satan has been waiting for! **Satan recognizes that no one who has had an addiction to** *crack* **is able to maintain control for any beneficial, lengthy period of time after they start back drinking.** Mindful, he's patiently *"waiting for the right opportunity"*, the chance to catch you under the influence of alcohol with the motive of deceptively awakening the desire and cravings for crack cocaine.

HE'S WANTS YOU TO THINK THAT YOU'RE STRONG ENOUGH TO HANDLE IT

In case you are that someone who has recently overcome or struggling to overcome crack cocaine I need for you to understand that if you start back drinking start, believing that you can handle casual drinking you will be giving Satan that *"opportune and favorable time"* he's been waiting for. My friend, don't fall victim to Satan's amusement. Luring you with alcohol is his way of *puffing you up* (Col.2:18; 8:1) with arrogance and blind confidence. I can't stress it enough dear reader, it is not morally wise — especially when it comes to the spiritual battle and deliverance from crack cocaine — to indulge in the gratification's of alcohol because of the possibility of its effect triggering or awaking the demon and desire for crack cocaine.

Try to make wiser choices when it comes to extracurricular activities. Instead of dwelling on drinking, get involved in things like going to *poetry readings, bowling, lifting weights, jogging,* just to name a few. **ABOVE ALL, GET INVOLVED IN CHURCH ACTIVITIES OR VOLUNTEERING FOR A WORTHY CAUSE.**

As the writer of Proverbs put it, "Wine is a mocker, strong drink (liquor) is raging: and whosoever is deceived therby is not wise" (Prov.20:1).

You Too Can Learn From King Solomon's Mistakes

King Solomon, being the *wisest* man of his time came to find out that **"drinking"** and applying **"spiritual wisdom"** are *enemies* of each other. He responds:

"I was a teacher, was king over Israel in Jerusalem. I spent all my time studying. I use my wisdom to check out everything... In fact, I'm now wiser than anyone who ruled over Jerusalem in the past. Then I used my mind to understand what it really means to be wise. AND I WANTED TO KNOW WHAT FOOLISH PLEASURE IS ALL ABOUT. I said to myself, "...I'll put foolish pleasure to the test... And what can pleasure do for me?" I TRIED CHEERING MYSELF UP BY DRINKING WINE. I even tried living in a foolish way... There wasn't any pleasure that I refused to give myself... But then I looked over everything... And nothing had any meaning. It was like chasing the wind. Nothing was gained... Meaningless!

And here's the final thing I want to say. Have respect for God and obey his commandments. That's what every human being should do. God will judge everything people do. That includes everything they try to hide (like drinking and drugs, sexual immorality...). HE'LL JUDGE EVERYTHING,

WHETHER IT'S GOOD OR EVIL" (Eccl. 1:12-13, 16b-17; 2:1-3a, 10-11; 12:8, 13-14 NIV).

Solomon, with all his wisdom, **through trial and error finally realized he was not able to make correct choices, judge properly, or truly exercise spiritual intelligence while under the influence of alcohol.**

He came to the conclusion that it was to no avail. **"Vanity of vanities, saith the Preacher, vanity of vanities; all is vanity"**. In other words Solomon is saying, *"I had to learn the hard way, and that's why I'm sharing this with you. It's nonsense! And if you want to be even wiser it's best to avoid the deceptions of alcohol, especially if you're a recovering addict".*

As I said before, my friend, the reason why you should not contemplate the idea is because there is always the possibility of the alcohol effect influencing or awakening the craving for crack and other drugs. Not to mention the main reason: *It causes people to forget their position in Christ.*

The prophet Isaiah confirms this by showing an illustration of a few respectful leaders of Israel who were deceived by the influence of alcohol. He records, **"Priest and prophets stumble because they are drunk. THEIR MINDS ARE TO CONFUSED** *to receive God's messages or give honest decisions"* (Isa.28: 7 CEV).

PRIEST AND PROPHETS STUMBLE BECAUSE THEY ARE DRUNK. THEIR MINDS ARE TO CONFUSED...

Elsewhere he writes, *"Woe (a curse or calamity) unto them that are mighty to drink wine and men of strength to mix strong drink"* (Isa.5: 22). The prophet Hosea adds, *"Whoredom and wine and new wine take away the heart"* (Hos.4: 11).

It's plain and simple: **Drinking alcohol distorts spiritual judgment**. It places the individual's deliverance in jeopardy, *"trapping people who have barely escaped from living the wrong kind of life"* (2Pet. 2:18, CEV). Drinking, it's a trap, my friend!

Drinking Makes You Forget Your Responsibilities To God

Let me be the first to confess that I, like Solomon, thought that after the Lord had given me the wisdom to recognize the many faces and tactics of the enemy, that when it came to drinking, if I carefully screened my alcohol intake I could remain in control. Well, after trial and error, like Solomon, I soon realized that it was just another trick of the enemy's. I too, with all my wisdom fell under the same *"spirit of deception"*. And deception is one of Satan's most potent weapons according to Genesis 3:1, and Revelations 19:20; 20:8, 10.

I found out that each time I convinced myself that I was in control of the situation and indulged in a simple beer, that its *"subtlety"* (Gen.3: 1) awaken the demon of strong drink (liquor), and it awaken another, which was the demon of crack cocaine influence. Please, please, don't deceive yourself any longer. The battle that you are in is none like any other! All you have to do is take a good look at reality and the rising crack epidemic around you. It is estimated that in 2002, 2.0 million persons (0.9 percent) were current cocaine users. 567,000 of who used crack during the same time period (0.2 percent), according to SAMHSA, Office of Applied Studies, National Survey on Drugs Use and Health, 2002

That was in 2002, could you imagine what the numbers are now? Well, it's much higher! And it all starts out with the gateway drug which is **Alcohol.** Remember, when it comes to temptation that deception is the name of the game when dealing with Satan. **Notice in Matthew 4:1-11 that after 40 days and nights of fasting that it was only when Jesus was physically weak that Satan came to tempt him. Well,** that's the same course of action that Satan considers when he decides to tempt us: he focuses on our physical needs, desires, and weaknesses.

However, Jesus responded, *"It is written..."* followed by the appropriated verses of scripture which unexpectedly were quotes from Deuteronomy 8:3 and 6:16. **We too can overcome our temptations to use drugs, drink, steal, commit sexual immoralities, and other sins by using the recourses Jesus used, "the written word of God!"**

When we permit God's word to determine our choices, we too will experience victory! Jesus' example of defeating temptation, Satan by appropriate scripture is a guideline for all mankind to follow when tempted. As an incentive *"fasting combined with the power of prayer"* (see Matt.17:21) give us more of an advantage. They are proper means for taping in or drawing upon God's divine power to assist us. *FASTING MUST BE JOINED WITH PRAYER, TO SUBDUE THE BODY.*

SCENARIO

Satan will try to deceive you by saying things like:

"Friend, you deserve a pat on the back. You haven't had a drink or use drugs in quite a while. You're no longer living on the streets; you've got a steady job, and a good mate. I'm proud of you. You have out done yourself! You don't hang around influential company anymore, you've changed a lot of your old bad habits, you even talk different, and you've been going to Church on a regular basis, and to rehab meetings. You are definitely in control!"

"You finally made a liar out of all those who said you'd never amount to anything. It's been a lot of hard work, and I know it has not been easy, all things being considered, but when are you going to start back enjoying yourself a little. I mean, there's nothing wrong with taking a little drink every now and then . You deserve it. God doesn't condemn a man for

drinking and enjoying all his hard work. He just condemns getting drunk, and you're not going to let that happen anymore, because you are in control!" There's nothing to worry about anymore, because you've learned from past experiences that you can only drink one or two beers and that's your limit. So what's there to be concern about? Have a good time, just be careful."

POWER PRAYER

I mmediately respond, it is written, **"Wine is a mocker, strong drink is raging: and whosoever is deceived thereby is not wise"** (Pro.20: 1).

Now in your words *say something like: Demonic, influential spirit of alcohol I rebuke you in the name of Jesus! If I were to drink beer, wine, or liquor, it's only giving you, Satan, a chance to ridicule or make mockery my spiritual walk. Alcohol makes people ignorant and sometimes violent. Therefore, I refuse to give in to its deception, because to do so would be unwise. In the mighty name of Jesus, I pray. Now thanks be unto God, which always causes us to triumph in Christ, (2Cor.2: 14). Amen.*

Option

It is written, **"It is not for kings (anyone in a position of leadership)... to drink wine, nor for princes strong drink (liquor): Lest they drink, and forget the law, and pervert the judgment of any of the afflicted"** (Pro.31: 4-5).

The Contemporary English Version reads, **"Kings and leaders should not get drunk or even want to drink. DRINKING MAKES YOU FORGET YOUR**

142

RESPONSIBILITIES... (as a warrior for Christ against the demonic forces of evil).

Now in your own words, *say something like: Glory to God. Now I understand, Lord. You are simply saying that people, like myself—with all my dirty laundry—whom God has called to be a leader—be it a leader in the work place or home—have an obligation to You, and an image of representation to uphold unto the Lord.*

I realize now that alcohol only distorts devout reasoning. It causes people who are seeking deliverance to make many shameful, ignorant, and unjust decisions. It also deceives people into using (crack), by making them believe that they are in control. It causes people to forget their responsibilities as leaders in the home and workplace. This in many cases has caused the person to lose their job, or experience a break up in their marriage. Today I've made up my mind to not allow the spirit of alcoholism to deceive any longer. I am more than a conqueror through Christ who lives in me.

"Now thanks be unto God, which always causeth us to triumph in Christ. Amen" (2 Cor. 2: 14).

Option

It is written: **"But as the days of Noah were, so shall also the coming of the son of man be... before the flood they were eating drinking... And knew not until the flood came... Watch, therefore; for ye know not what hour your Lord doth come... But and if that evil servant say in his heart, My lord delayeth his coming; And...begin to eat and drink with the drunkards, the lord...shall come... when he looketh not for him... And shall cut asunder...his portion with the hypocrites; (shall send him to hell with all the other hypocrites).** Matt. 24:37-39, 42, 48-51

Now in your own words, *say something like: Praise God. For today I'm going to watch, be ready and waiting for the coming of my Lord! I'm not going to be high or drunk; I'm going to be in my right state of mind. Lord, I*

143

understand the verse completely now. What you're saying is that I'd better not be high or drunk when you come for me, or else.

I confess, Lord, that every now and then I do get the taste for alcohol, therefore I'm asking you to take that urge and taste out of my mouth, right now, in your mighty and precious name. Lord, I realize now that when those urges arise it's only my flesh (the alcohol demon) crying out, having a tantrum like a little child who wants to have its way. In the name of Jesus I command my flesh (the selfish child) to cease from those tantrums and calm down! You are not having your way anymore!

Satan, I'm not going to let you deceive me any longer. I can't afford to keep taking chances, dabbling in sin as the people in the days of Noah did: They were drinking and partying, committing fornication, adultery, and much more, before they realized that the appointed time (of death) was upon them. And the end result was that "they were sent to hell with the rest of the hypocrites" (Matt.24: 51).

Praise God, it's not going to happen to me. I'm on to you Satan. I've learned to stop saying to myself "my Lord delayeth his coming", like I use to and get high at will. I don't want to be in the clubs, the crack house, or anywhere else getting high or drunk and my time comes. If I die in such a state of mind or environment my eternal home will indeed be with the hypocrites. Praise God, I am free from the demonic influence of drugs and alcohol, in Jesus name. Amen.

12

Prayers Not To Prostitute Oneself Or Solicit

When it comes to deliverance from crack cocaine addiction Satan will deceptively make **men** and ***women*** disregard the sin of whoredom and whoremongering. The devil will **make a man think** that he is able to keep the company of a crack whore, prostitute simply for sexual pleasures and not give in to the temptation to use.

The enemy of the church, Satan (Matt.13:39) will also ***deceive women*** *into prostituting themselves and giving oral sex* for a measly hit of crack or money to purchase the drug. Please women, stop allowing yourselves to be belittled to the point of whoredom, subjecting yourselves to diseases like aids, mouth sores and other sexual diseases, *because prostitution and whoredom is one of the worst acts that you can commit against God (see 2Kg. 9:22; Jer.3:2; Ezek. 16:28-30)* and the Bible confirms, *"...No other sin clearly affects the body as this one does"* (1Cor. 6:18-20 NLT). And since the devil knows that *"whores and whoremongers will spend eternity in the lake that burns with fire and sulfur, hell"* according to Revelation 21:8 he will do all he can to keep them from repenting.

Dear reader, even if you're a woman who is dating or living with a man and you two are having sex but not married to each other **"and he helps you with bills,** *or gives you money and gifts God still see this as the sin of whoredom, prostituting yourself"* (Ezek.16:32-34).

Satan knows that statement to be true because *"he knows scripture"* (see Lk. 4:9-11; Ps. 91:11) and realizes that the Written Word of God says, "...no whoremonger, whore, fornicator, adulterer or homosexual will have any inheritance in the kingdom of God and Christ." (See Eph. 5:5; 1Cor. 6:9-10)

Please, daughter, don' be like "the woman Jezebel who God **GAVE TIME TO REPENT** from sexual immorality BUT SHE REFUSED and suffered the punishment! (See Rev. 2:20-23).

And men, don't be deceived into surrounding yourself in the company of such women, because nine times out of ten you will end up sharing the drug right along with her even if your intention is not to use but to simply to receive a sexual favor from her because, the **"SPIRIT OF DECEPTION"** that possesses the whore is more powerful than you think.

To verify that statement there's a passage in the bible that talks about the **"tares and wheat". THE TARES** are the people that *Satan plants* in the church to cause confusion, division and pull *would-be Christians*, which are **the wheat**, away from the gospel, thereby, causing them to slip up and sin. ((See Matt.13:24-30,39-42

In reference to **"THE SPIRIT OF DECEPTION BEING SO POWERFUL",** The Scofield Study Bible, footnotes on Matthew 13:24-30 confirms, "The wheat of God at once becomes the scene of Satan's activity. Where children of the kingdom are gathered, there, among the wheat, Satan sows children of the wicked "who profess to be children of the kingdom, and in outward ways appear to be true children of God, that only the angel in the end can be trusted to separate them (vv.40-42).

146

SO GREAT IS SATAN'S POWER OF DECPTION that **"THE TARES"** (the people Satan uses to his to disrupt God's work in the church) **ARE OFTEN DECEIVED INTO THINKING** that they are true children of the kingdom" (*See Matt.13:14 Scofield Study Bible, footnotes*).

My friend, **if Satan can deceive "his children"** (1Jn.3:10; Jn.8:44), those he's actually using to disrupt the church **into believing for a moment that they are God's children,** when he is actually using them to disrupting the church, **then by the "SAME POWER OF DECEPTION" he gets people to believe** that certain companions will not hinder or disrupt their deliverance when God's word specifies, *"Be not deceived, my friend, evil company corrupts good character"* (1Cor.15:33).

God also adds, **"I will punish both parties for their wicked ways. They engage in prostitution...because they have deserted the Lord to give themselves to prostitution. Alcohol (drugs) and prostitution have robbed them of their brains, took away their understanding...FOR THE SPIRIT OF WHOREDOMS HATH CAUSED THEM TO ERR...they have gone a whoring from under their God"**. (See Hos.4:9-12 TNIV).

"Keep...away from the smooth talk of a wayward woman, an adulterous woman. Do not lust in your heart after her... He who embraces her will not go unpunished" (Prov.6:24-29 NLT).

The Devil Will Whisper Things To You Like: *"Well, you finally got this crack habit licked. I'm proud of you. But it's been a while since you've been with a woman or man. You've been doing well. You've been going to Church, Bible study and all that good stuff".*

"But ever since your wife, husband, girlfriend or boyfriend... decided to leave because they didn't understand what you were going through, the dating game has past you by. If you don't hurry up and get back into the flow of things

you're going to end up growing old all alone. Aren't you tired of being alone? Tired of waiting for that so-called right one? Tired of being rejected when you think you've found that right one?"

"It's time for you to stop depriving yourself of companionship. Stop sitting around feel sorry for yourself, waiting for love. You know what to do. You've been out there before. Put your game face on. Go out tonight and find somebody to satisfy you.

"Those crack-whores are still out there. Go find you one tonight. Buy her some drugs or pay her straight out. Then get her to fulfill your desires. When she finishes simply go your separate ways. It's that simple. And stop worrying, you won't be deceived again into using. Remember, you're stronger now and I'm proud of you. Let's do this!"

Does this sound familiar? Well, as sure as the anointing power of the Holy Spirit is inspiring these pages I can assure you that if you give in to Satan's suggestions of sexual immorality **there's a 99 percent chance that you will end up using too.** That's why Satan's trying to deceive you.

The reason the odds are in Satan's favor that you will most likely end up using is because **ALL "Crack Whores, Prostitutes and Adulterers "ARE POSSESSED"** (Lk.8: 36) **BY THE DEMONIC "SPIRIT OF WHOREDOM"** (Hos. 4:12; 5:4 NRSV).

This spirit's main function is to **entice, seduce and attract men** (Prov.7:9-13) with the purpose of causing them **"TO FOLLOW HER LIKE AN OX ON THE WAY TO BE SLAUGHTERED"** (Prov.7:22) *thereby causing them to STRAY away from living a life that pleases God.*

"Such a woman has caused the destruction of a lot of men. Her house is the way to hell!" (Prov.7:27 TEV).

Satan Has A Motive For Possessing and Using Whore's And Prostitutes

What I'm trying to get you to realize, dear reader, is that **ANY CONDUCT OF SEX OUTSIDE THE COMMAND OF MARRIAGE GOD WILL "JUDGE" AS AN ACT OF WHOREDOM!** And God plainly says that "no whores or whoremongers, adulterers, fornicators, or homosexuals) *will be allowed to enter the kingdom of heaven*" (1 Cor.6:9-10; Eph.5: 5-6; Rev. 21:7-8; 22:15).

Although the sexual immoral woman may not realize it, but she has answered the casting call of Satan's to assist him in his pursuit to bring all those who surrender to her advances into the bowels of hell. (See Pro.7: 27; 9:18; 5:5; Rev.21:8; 22:15):

Dear Reader, if you are participating in any sinful acts such as *prostitution*, ***fornication, adultery, whoredom,*** or ***whoremongering*** (*soliciting the company of prostitutes*), I beg you to immediately *repent* of this abomination or else be prepared to receive the punishments that's waits. **"He who embraces her will not go unpunished!"**(Pro.6:29 NLB).

A Point To Remember

Prostitution is often referred to as ***"the oldest profession."*** Indeed, it has always been a common way for women to make money, even in Bible times. The Bible tells us that ***prostitution is immoral*** according to Proverbs 23:27-28. **God forbids involvement with prostitutes because He knows such involvement is detrimental to both men and women.** Prostitution not only destroys marriages, families, and lives, but it destroys the spirit and soul in a way that leads to physical and spiritual death. *"The body is not for sexual immorality but for the Lord...and not to be joined to a prostitute, because*

149

if a man joins himself with a prostitute, he becomes one with her" (1Cor.6:15-17 NLT).

The good news is that just like anyone else, **prostitutes have the opportunity to receive salvation and eternal life from God, to be cleansed of all their unrighteousness and be given a brand new life!** **All they must do is turn away from their sinful lifestyle** and *turn to the living God,* whose grace and mercy are boundless. Remember when Jesus told the lady, "**TO SIN NO MORE**" (Jn.8:1-11) after she was about to be stoned for sexual immorality? Well, he giving that opportunity to woman today that will take heed and change from their sexual immoral lifestyle.

Do Men See Me As A Pathetic Sinful Whorish Silly Woman

When the Apostle Paul addressed the issue of **silly women** not only was he referring to those women back then who were being deceived and used by men who claimed to be sent by God and took advantage of their *vulnerability,* but Paul is referring to **ALL women, back then and now, who are so easily taken advantage of, deceive and seduced by drugs, money, material things and other offers that men make to lure or entice them into in sexual immorality.** Their purpose is gain control over **weak-willed women, who are loaded down with sins and are swayed by all kinds of evil desires"** (2Tim.3:6). The Cambridge Dictionary says that a silly weak-willed woman is "**a woman with WEAK MORAL PRINCIPLES; a woman who is easily to adopt another person's opinion.**"

When most whoremongering men are on the prowl they're not looking for a woman with the intent of helping her grow, excel in spiritual strength and

150

character; they're not looking for a woman who has her own opinion about things and stands on that opinion. **They're looking for persona that tells them that the woman does not have a lot of knowledge about God's word;** a woman who's opinion can be easily swayed, a woman who with little convincing will adapt to their way of thinking, a woman who lets them think for them, a woman who can't make up her mind when it comes to difficult situations and will turn to drugs or alcohol to fix the problem a woman who will and literary will allow a man to be in control.

Women Learn to Recognize These Men

When most people hear someone say that another person is *weak* or *silly* they automatically assume that the person being talked about is someone who can't rationally think for themselves, lacks common sense and the ability to make self-confident decisions. According to Webster Dictionary it's an accurate definition and that's why Paul, in 2 Tim.3:1-6 was merely trying to point out areas that most women *emotionally and spiritually have struggles in* so that they won't continue to fall victim to egotistical men who view them as a woman who can be easily swayed, or weak willed. There are always *weak-minded* women in every community and household and to the devil and those with his spirit such women are more than appealing to them! Why, because the enemy knows **that "silly women are easily flattered, they lend a willing ear to anything that has the appearance of financial gain, and their hearts are open to anything that promises to advance their welfare.**

151

Again, most men who are in the market for inane women **talk a lot about themselves** and what **they** want; they curse repeatedly without consideration of others; they **brag** about themselves, they **find fault** and criticize the opinion of others and think that their plan is the best plan, they have leisure, money, or at least **claim to** have; they move about clandestinely in society and by their activities they obtain a certain degree of **influence over the naive** and weak minded. The know that the last thing a weak willed, spiritually uninformed woman wants **is to cut off from the love** of family and close friends and so when they run across a woman with such a problem they will use the woman's pain and emotional retardation to their advantage.

Now, you might say, *"I'm not stupid, silly or weak willed. I do the things I do because I have to"*. Well, to those who are looking to promote *their own sense of self* it's a sign of weakness and vulnerability to them. That's why **it's your responsibility to get a spiritual and rational grip on what the world calls the game of life!** You do this by first *being real with yourself* and *admitting* the areas of your life that you know without a doubt you're being taken advantage of in by your love ones and stop playing the fool! You know what's going on around you! I know that somewhere deep down inside of you there's a woman that's tired of selling her body, being used and abused, neglected, disrespected, thought of as being dumb and stupid! A woman that's tired of humiliating herself, tired of having to sleep with or perform the favor of oral sex for a measly crumb of crack cocaine.

Woman Where's Your Dignity

Somewhere deep inside there's an **intelligent, stable** person and homemaker that wants to be respected and appreciated for being smart, strong and able to make logically decisions. My friend, that person who is waiting to express himself is **God's Holy Spirit**. The **"Spirit of intelligence"** (1Jn.2:27) and **"boldness"** (Eph.6:19-20) **that's living in you** is the only Person that nobody can manipulate according to 1st John 2:27, and if he can't be manipulated then after you make him your **"comforter"** neither will you be so **easily swayed by sin!** (See Jn.16:8).

Pray for God to send you a husband! Tell Him that you're tired of living the sinful life! The Lord has promised, **"And I will give you pastors, according to mine heart, which shall feed you with knowledge and understanding** (Jer.3:15). When God said, **"I will give you a pastor"** He was also referring to a **godly husband** with loving, pastoral qualities because the office of pastor or leadership begins with the character of a husband towards his wife and family according to 1st Timothy 3:12 and 1st Corinthians 14:35. My friend, when you **repent a**nd begin to **acknowledge and request** God's help in matters such as intimacy He will send you a mate who will be more concern about your salvation and happiness than he would be for his own sexual gratifications.

You Don't Have To Live Like That You Are A Child Of God's Not Satan's

In the book of 1st John 3:8-10, Deuteronomy 32:5 and John 8:44 we find the writers discussing the distinguished character of **"THE CHILDREN OF THE DEVIL, AND THE CHILDREN OF GOD".** In addition, we find the discussion of **"the blessing that fall upon the children of God,** those who depend, trust, and obey God" (see Dt.28:1-14), and "the calamity, misfortune of the children of the devil, those who try to create their destiny, outside of God's will" (See Dt.28: 15-45, 60-62).

As a child of God's, a follower of Christ's we are supposed to stoop to the level of desperation that folk who don't know God do in order to make a dollar. When Moses led Israel out of bondage from under the Egyptian, God gave Moses regulations to administer to them **concerning forbidden sex practices.** "The Lord said to Moses, say this to your people... do not act like the people in Egypt, where you use to live, or act like the people in Canaan where I'm taking you. You must not imitate their way of life. You must never have sex with a close relative...your mother...your sister and half-sisters... your aunt... with both a woman and her daughter... or practice homosexuality... do not defile yourselves by doing any of these things". "Do not defile your daughter by making her a prostitute, or the land will be filled with detestable wickedness (Lev: 18:1-30; 19:29 NLT).

My friend, just as **"God gave the whore, Jezebel, and the men who slept with her time to change, repent,** for their sinful ways but she refused, which was a wrong choice"** (see Rev2:20-23), I pray that you won't make the erroneous choice she made and *suffer eternity* in a place that was originally *"prepared for the devil and his angels"* (Matt.25:41), but now has been reserved for and all of mankind *"who choose not to repent of evil"* (Rev.20:12-15; 19:20; Matt.13:37-42; 25: 31-34,46).

God is not in favor of sending anyone to hell, but he will not allow the stain of prostitution or

154

whormongering (soliciting the service of a whore) to breach the gates of the heavenly city (Rev.21:1, 7, 8, 24, 27). **"Blessed are they that do his commandments that they may have the right...to enter in through the gates of the city. But OUTSIDE the city are the sexual immoral...WHORES, whoremongers...and all who love to live a lie"** (Rev.22:15).

Today, God is giving you **"a chance to return from your evil ways"** (Jer.18:11; 24:7). Remember, **"It's not God's wish or plan for any of us to die, perish and go to hell, so he is giving people time for everyone to repent".** (See 2Pet.3:9 NLT).

Will you repent? Will you accept your heavenly Father's plea for you to **"please stop prostituting, committing whoredom, and whoremongering? Will you renounce that evil spirit in the name of Jesus!"**

PRAYER

Prayer FOR THE WOMAN To Rebuke The Spirit of Prostitution

*"Dear God, according to 1ˢᵗ John 1:9 you said that **if I confess my sins** of fornication, adultery, prostitution and whoredom that You will be faithful and just to **forgive me**. Well, I confess my sins... I've made a lot of painstaking, ungodly choices concerning intimacy and I need your help. I realize now that Satan has been **"using me to draw men into the belly of hell"** (Pro. 7:5, 13, 22, 27; 9:13-18; 2:18). Lord, I'm tired of being hurt, used and abused. I'm tired of living this way. I'm tired of disappointing You and **"true blessing passing me by"** (Jer.5:25).*

*I don't want to continue **"taking life for granted"** (Ps.10:4, 11) "go to sleep tonight and **unfortunately*** *wake up in hell tomorrow"* (Lk.16:22-23). *So I repent of this sin (Rev.2:20-22) and ask You, Lord, to send me a husband, "a man after Your own heart" (Acts 13:22 and 2Chr.19:3). Lord, I enjoy sex and you said that "if I couldn't contain myself that it's better for me to marry than to burn" (1Cor.7:9), and "to avoid the punishment of sexual sin let every man have is his own wife and every woman have her own husband" (1Cor.7:2). Lord, I don't want to spend "eternity in hell because of sexual immorality" (1Cor.6:9; Rev.2:3; 21:8; 22:15), so I'm asking You, Lord, to please, please send me a husband. Thank you. Amen".*

PRAYER

Prayer FOR THE MAN To Renounce The Evil Spirit Of Prostitute Soliciting

It is written, "For the lips of a strange woman drop as honeycomb, and her mouth is smoother than oil. But her end is bitter as wormwood (a sour tasting plant)... Her feet go down to death; her steps take hold of hell... **REMOVE THY WAY FAR FROM HER, AND COME NOT NEAR THE DOOR OF HER HOUSE... HER HOUSE IS THE WAY TO HELL.** (Pro.5: 3-5, 8; 6:25-26; 7:27). Also the Word of God declares, "He that overcometh shall inherit all things... But the fearful (those who turn away from God), and unbelieving, and abominable... **AND WHOREMONGERS**... shall have their part in the lake which burneth with fire and brimstone" (Rev.21: 7-8).

"For this ye know, **THAT NO WHOREMONGER**... (a person who seeks the company of a prostitute)hath any inheritance in the kingdom of Christ and God" (Eph.5: 5).

Now in your own words pray something like: *Demon spirit of whoredom, prostitution, fornication, or adultery, I rebuke you "in the name of Jesus!" (Acts3:*

6). I will not allow you to deceive me into seeking the companionship of a whore, or to continue in this promiscuous, fornicating, adulteress relationship. For my will be bitter because God's word tells me that a whore's house is the doorway to hell. And that's exactly where I will end up if I continue to listen to you Satan, and remain in this predicament or relationship.

The Word of God implies that **"whoremongers... (fornicators and adulterers) shall have their part in the lake which burneth with fire"** (Rev.21: 8).

For years, ignorant of your abilities, Satan, I allow you to instill feelings of loneliness, abandonment, rejection, and unimportance, which caused me to give in to sexual immorality. I realize now that it is a sin against God, and my body, which is the temple of the Holy Ghost (1Cor.6: 19). Therefore it's a sin to lay down with a whore, or participate in any other sexual relationships outside the guidelines of marriage. (See 1Cor.7: 8-9).

The Word plainly tells me that adulterers and fornicators—**which is the same as whoredom**—will not inherit the kingdom of God (1Cor.6: 9). And now that I am aware of this truth I can no longer continue to **"jeopardize losing my inheritance"**, **"the place that has been prepared for me in heaven"** (Jn.14:2), **"or my rewards from God for overcoming evil suggestion"** (Js.1:12). From this day on I will wait on the Lord to bless me with a suitable mate. I repent and change my ways. Thank you, Lord, for your plans to bless me.

Thank you for opening my eyes dear, Lord. Thank you for showing me in the Word, that if I was to continue in the deceptive by the sinful ways of fornication, adultery, or whoredom that I would eventually spending eternity in hell. Lord, I also understand now that when it comes to the sin of adultery (sleeping with another man's wife or vice versa) that there is a more TERRIBLE punishment awaiting those who don't repent according to 1st Thessalonians 4:6.

The Bible clearly states that all "fornicators and whoremongers...shall have their part in the lake which burneth with and brimstone" (Rev.21: 8).

In the name of Jesus Christ, I bind every thought of adultery, fornication, whoredom, and any other thoughts of sexual immorality. Shut up, **SUGGESTIVE DEMON SPIRIT OF WHOREDOM.** In the name of Jesus, I will not give in to your immoral voice. It is your purpose, Satan, to carve a pathway into the pits of hell for me. Possibly by killing me tonight while I'm out seeking drugs and immoral companionship, or maybe by exposing me to aids or some other deadly sexual disease.

Lord, I know that you'd rather I would get married because Your word says, **"it is not good for man to be alone" (Gen.2: 18),** and **"to avoid fornication let every man have his own wife, and let every woman have her own husband" (1Cor.7: 2).**

Therefore, I thank you, dear God, for my future wife/husband who you will bless me with so that I will not continue to sin against thee. Lord, I know you will answer my prayer and I will wait on thee. Amen. In Jesus Name I pray. Amen. . Praise the Lord!

Never Give Up Your Quest For You Deliverance

Dear friend, before concluding this book there's one thing that I always want you to remember. And that is, no matter how many times you fall in your quest for deliverance, or how many times other people criticize you for falling, never gives up trying!

I remember one time when I fell and my mother said to me, "You ought to stop playing with God". My response to her was, "Mother, I'm not playing with God. It's like to forces are at a tug of war with me. It's like God is pulling me by the right arm and the devil is pulling me by my left arm. So, if I listen to you and throw down my Bible, I might as well Satan that he has won".

Therefore, I can't give up fighting. I've got to keep trying no matter how insincere it may seem to you and others because I truly want to be free!"

Well, because I didn't give up when others criticized me, 1 am free! My suggestion to you, friend, is when you fall, don't just lie there wallowing in the mud of condemnation, depression, and sorry. Get up, dust yourself off, and get back in the saddle. **"A RIGHTEOUS PERSON MAY FALL SEVEN TIMES, BUT HE GETS UP AGAIN"** (Pro.24: 16 TEV).

It may seem like a rough ride, and you'll probably get thrown a few more times. But if you keep getting up, and getting back on (the Word of God), I promise that you will *break* that habit. Ride is, Cowboy.

And now may the God of peace, who brought again from the dead our Lord Jesus, equip you with all you need for doing his will. May he...produce in you through the power of Christ (the Word) all that is well pleasing to him" (Heb. 13:20-21).

Remind God of the promise to "bring you out from under such burdens, to rid you from

159

the bondage, and redeem you with and outstretched arm (Ex.6:6).

God has given us *"all power over our adversary, Satan, and the authority as believers to speak the written word over the entanglement and bondages of life"* according to Luke 10:19, Mark 11:23; 3:27 and Matthew16:19. 1st John 5:14, tells us that *"if we ask anything according to God's will for our lives he will answer our prayers accordingly".*

Therefore, you must realize that it is not God's will for you to be a drug addict, alcoholic, homeless, a prostitute, in an abusive relationship or marriage, jobless, sick, a fornicator or adulterer. In that case it's up to you to find out what the Word, the promises of God have to say about such events, and declare, *"It is written"*, followed by the appropriate verse over those situations just as Jesus did in Luke 4:1-12. And afterwards you can be sure that God's word will bring about positive results as promised.

Dear reader, I want you to realize that Satan is afraid of you! And that's the reason he wants to keep you under the influence of drugs, alcohol, and in the company of the heathen. He knows that as long as you're under the influence that you'll never come to the realization of who you are in Christ and the power you have over him to become that testimony, witness and upstanding person that God intended for you to be from your day of birth. But praise to God! Those fears which Satan has had of you becoming that person which God intended from your day of birth are about to come true. Yes, you're, on the way to becoming that person that the enemy has been afraid of for so many years! **"Crack cocaine let my people go so that they may serve God!"** (Ex.8:1, 20).

The End

About The Author

Willie J. Henderson, graduate from Christian Charismatic Methodist Bible Training Center. For years I too was lost in the world of drug abuse, sin, misery, and misfortune. The demonic spirit of self-centeredness and rebellion had a hold on my life for 20 long years as I struggled with crack cocaine and its counterparts. But one particular day I opened my Bible and was led to Ephesians 6:12, Revelation 12:7-17, John 14:30 and Luke 4:1-12. It was in those chapters that God's Holy Spirit revealed to me who was causing all the pandemonium in my life, and how to follow the example that Jesus set for mankind by speaking the Word of God over those assaults as instructed in Luke 4:1-12).

My friend, just as the woman with the issue of blood touched the hem of Jesus' garment and was healed (Matt.9:18-22), when you touched this anointed book of deliverance, **the Spirit of God resting on these pages began its healing process in your life. Because where the Spirit of the Lord is, there is freedom!** (1Cor.3:17).

Other Book By This Author and Ministry Include:

1. Crack Cocaine Let My People Go Appropriate Prayer Results In Deliverance.
2. Crack Cocaine Evil Spirit In Jesus name I Command You To Release Your Hold
3. BooBoo's true Story The Lil Crackhead Boy Returns To God

4. Woman Ya Gotta Know When Enough Is Enough; When To let Go And let God

5. The trials of a Lil Girl Who Didn't Listen To Her Mama; Veda's True Story

Made in United States
Orlando, FL
04 July 2024

48593839R00089